FOOD POLITICS
WHAT EVERYONE NEEDS TO KNOW

FOOD POLITICS
WHAT EVERYONE NEEDS TO KNOW

ROBERT PAARLBERG

OXFORD
UNIVERSITY PRESS

2010

OXFORD
UNIVERSITY PRESS

Oxford University Press, Inc., publishes works that further
Oxford University's objective of excellence
in research, scholarship, and education.

Oxford   New York
Auckland   Cape Town   Dar es Salaam   Hong Kong   Karachi
Kuala Lumpur   Madrid   Melbourne   Mexico City   Nairobi
New Delhi   Shanghai   Taipei   Toronto

With offices in
Argentina   Austria   Brazil   Chile   Czech Republic   France   Greece
Guatemala   Hungary   Italy   Japan   Poland   Portugal   Singapore
South Korea   Switzerland   Thailand   Turkey   Ukraine   Vietnam

Copyright © 2010 by Oxford University Press, Inc.

Published by Oxford University Press, Inc.
198 Madison Avenue, New York, New York 10016

www.oup.com

Oxford is a registered trademark of Oxford University Press.

Library of Congress Cataloging-in-Publication Data
Paarlberg, Robert L.
Food politics : what everyone needs to know / Robert Paarlberg.
p.   cm.
Includes bibliographical references and index.
ISBN 978-0-19-538960-9; 978-0-19-538959-3 (pbk.)
1. Agriculture and state.   2. Food supply.   3. Food—Marketing.
4. Nutrition policy.   I. Title.
HD1415.P12 2010
338.1'9—dc22   2009038334

1 3 5 7 9 8 6 4 2

Printed in the United States of America
on acid-free paper

CONTENTS

7 Food Aid and Food Power   **70**

8 The Politics of Obesity   **81**

12 Organic and Local Food   139

13 Food Safety and Genetically Engineered Food   155

ACKNOWLEDGMENTS

This book was for me an interesting departure. It was not undertaken to solve a specific research problem, it was not supported by a funding agency, and there was no coauthorship or collaboration with a narrow circle of colleagues. In writing this book, I found myself drawing instead on multiple resources developed over my own lengthy career of research, consulting, and more than a dozen years of annual preparations for a course I teach on food politics. Many colleagues have helped me enormously along the way, probably with no idea it would ever lead to a book of this kind. Providing anything like a complete list of acknowledgments becomes out of the question.

I can, however, acknowledge several sources of constant help over all this time. Wellesley College has been my valued teaching home since 1976. This institution gives me generous research support whenever I need it and classroom access to some of the world's smartest and most talented young women. The friend who made my career at Wellesley possible, Lawrence Sullivan, is someone I cannot thank too often or too much. The Weatherhead Center for International Affairs at Harvard University is a second institutional home for me, a place to collaborate with world-class scholars and international affairs practitioners from scores of different countries. Here it is appropriate for me to mention the personal association I have treasured most at Harvard, with Stanley Hoffmann, a humane scholar and teacher who never had any particular reason to help me out, but did so anyway over the years because that has always been his nature. My third institutional home has been the International Food Policy Research Institute (IFPRI) in Washington, D.C., where I have enjoyed a diverse mix of research and consulting opportunities. My most valued connection here is with Rajul Pandya-Lorch, a careful and tireless presence, who manages to keep IFPRI's door open to my work and who always seems to know whom I should be in touch with in Nairobi, Delhi, or Beijing.

I also owe a continuing debt to Michael Lipton, who has reserved surprising amounts of his valuable time at key moments for reading and reacting to what I have been writing and for tutoring me with his deeply informed understanding of rural poverty. Like so many others, I fail to measure up to Michael's high standards, but with gracious good cheer he helps me out anyway. Valued lessons in food and farming around the world have also come to me continuously through collaborations and coauthorships with Merilee Grindle, Robert Thompson, David Orden, Carl Pray, Ron Herring, and Calestous Juma. Particular gratitude in support of this new book must be extended to William Masters and Philip Paarlberg, who agreed on short notice to read the manuscript in draft and to provide reactions. I have learned to trust their judgment. It goes without saying, the mistakes that remain in this book are my own responsibility and nobody else's.

Special mention next goes to Lowell Hardin, an agricultural visionary and a humanitarian who provided essential support to my career in the early years when it mattered most. I learned later that Lowell has done this for countless others in the field and still does. Thanks, Lowell.

I also wish to thank my editor at Oxford University Press, Angela Chnapko, for originally suggesting this project and for guiding it to publication with a light but sure touch.

In the end, it is always family that matters most. This is particularly true in my case, as I was fortunate to be the son of one of the most respected agricultural policy experts of the second half of the 20th century, Don Paarlberg, from Purdue University. I dare not calculate how much less I would have done in my career without the constancy of his inspiration, example, and support. But wait, the Paarlberg family support system does not stop there! My father's younger brother, Hoey Paarlberg, and my cousin Philip Paarlberg are also agricultural specialists. Hoey grew up with my dad on a farm in Lake County, Indiana, and later managed farms for Purdue University. My conversations with Hoey have always been a learning experience as well as a great pleasure. Cousin Phil, meantime, is a widely published professor of agricultural economics at Purdue and the brains of the family. I am always flattered when mistaken for him.

My late brother, Don Paarlberg Jr., also played an important role in setting my career path. It was a 1967 trip to visit Don, who was then a Peace Corps volunteer in Nepal, that triggered my interest in international development and introduced me to the dramatic challenges facing Asia's rural poor. In addition, it was Don and his wife, Heeja, who introduced me and my own wife, Marianne, to the sensory pleasures of well-prepared Korean and Chinese food.

Marianne gets the last but strongest acknowledgment of all. During her own long career as the art director at a major university press, she taught me important lessons about how authors should and should not behave. And as a versatile chef, she also knows her way around food. Nutritious and well-prepared food was as important on her side of the family as successful farming was on mine. Together, we make a good combination.

PREFACE

When it comes to food, everybody is interested. Humorist Will Rogers opened his routine by saying, "I never met a man I didn't like." In my own life, I have never met a person who did not like food, either growing it, preparing it, tasting it, or in many cases, arguing about it. We all have strong opinions about food, just as we do about politics. Food issues that become political are thus doubly divisive.

For this reason, I hesitated when asked by Oxford University Press to write a book describing "what everyone needs to know" about food politics. For each issue I would cover, a number of readers with views opposed to my own would be offended. Food politics can be a realm of irreconcilable difference. For each issue, there would also be specialists better informed than I, ready to notice even the smallest error. With each topic covered, then, I would be angering one group of readers while revealing my limitations to the other.

What persuaded me to write this book was press coverage of the so-called world food crisis of 2008. When international food prices spiked upward sharply in the spring of that year, I was struck by the different stories told. Journalists reported that the world was running out of food. Environmentalists asserted that modern agricultural production methods had become unsustainable. Humanitarians warned that too much food was being diverted for use as transport fuel. Others said the problem was too many food imports by China. In fact, none of these popular explanations touched the core of the problem. The international food price spike was part of a temporary bubble in all commodity prices, oil and metals as well as food, a macroeconomic effect that was worsened inside the food sector by a series of national export bans and then panic buying triggered by those bans.

There was also public confusion over the consequences of the price spike. Did high prices on the world market really mean an additional 100 million people would now go hungry? Few seemed to appreciate that most food consumers around the world were largely insulated from international price fluctuations thanks to the restrictive trade policies of their governments (including the export bans that had amplified the spike). The export price of food is not the price most consumers pay. The "international" price of rice may have tripled, but rice consumers in China and in many other countries were not paying any more than before. I concluded that a book shedding light on these and other basics might be useful after all.

I also agreed to write this book in the hope of rebalancing some debates about food and farming. In recent years, a swelling body of popular literature has persuaded much of the attentive public, including many of my closest friends, that high-productivity farming based on specialization and modern science is a mistake. Popular writers now argue for a return to something like the farming and eating styles of an earlier era. Agricultural production should once again take place on small diversified farms rather than on large specialized farms. Soil nutrients should be replaced "organically" using composted animal manure without any synthetic nitrogen fertilizers. Food marketing systems should be more local and less international. The preparation and consumption of food should be slow rather than fast. These assertions that the best food will be organic, local, and slow require critical scrutiny by someone other than a journalist or a "food writer." Most of the academically trained specialists I have worked with—nutritionists, agricultural economists, toxicologists, biologists, soil scientists, and irrigation engineers—have serious reservations about these most recent food fashions. I decided it might be useful for Oxford's readers to learn why.

The information in this book has come to me from the published work of other academics plus my own lifetime of work among such specialists. For those with the appetite, a sampling of suggestions for further reading is at the end of the book. My credentials for writing this book include my discipline as a political scientist plus the considerable topical and geographic diversity of my research and published work. Over the course of my three-decade career, I have conducted research on food and agriculture in the United States, Europe, India, Bangladesh, China, Brazil, Argentina, and most recently, in more than a dozen countries in Africa. In doing this work, I operate as an independent scholar; I have never accepted corporate funding for any of my research. My work has been supported generously and continuously by my home institution, Wellesley College, and also by the Weatherhead Center for International Affairs at Harvard University, where I maintain a research affiliation. I have also received support on more than one occasion from the International Food Policy Research Institute (IFPRI), the U.S. Agency for International Development (USAID), the Council on Foreign Relations, the Brookings Institution, the Ford Foundation, the Rockefeller

Foundation, and the Bill and Melinda Gates Foundation. The conduct of independent scholarship in my field would not be possible without organizations such as these.

I first became interested in international food and agricultural policy immediately following my graduation from Carleton College in Minnesota in the summer of 1967. I took a marvelous trip to Nepal to visit my brother Don, who was working there as a Peace Corps volunteer. This early journey, from Singapore, to Kuala Lumpur, to Calcutta, and finally to Kathmandu, gave me a first-hand encounter with what Swedish economist Gunnar Myrdal was then calling an "Asian drama." Would food production in impoverished Asia keep pace with population growth or not? Fortunately, even as Myrdal was expressing his concerns, small farmers on irrigated lands were gaining access to the improved seeds and more productive techniques of the so-called green revolution. This technology upgrade soon transformed these countries from aid-dependent charity cases into thriving centers of increasing food production and rapid income growth. I wanted to learn more about these matters.

Today, the food drama is not in Asia but in sub-Saharan Africa, where most farmers do not yet have access to high-productivity methods. In Africa today, more than 60 percent of all citizens still live and work in the countryside as small farmers (most are women) or as animal herders. Because the productivity of their labor is so low, average income is only $1 a day, and one of three is chronically undernourished. Africa's population is still growing rapidly, so under a business-as-usual scenario, the number of undernourished people in sub-Saharan Africa will increase by another 30 percent by 2020. This will happen even if food prices on the world market are low.

Hunger problems of this kind are increasingly difficult for citizens in wealthy societies to comprehend. We now struggle with eating too much food rather than too little. In this book, the politics of food scarcity and food abundance get equal time.

Communicating useful information on food politics to an aware audience of nonspecialists is a challenging task. How much technical knowledge should be assumed? In addition, specialists often rely on terms of art that nonspecialists find unfamiliar and unhelpful. My own approach to this challenge has been shaped over the years by my work at Wellesley College, where every year I teach a multidisciplinary seminar on food and agricultural policy to an elite group of seniors. These students are smart, curious, hard working, and well traveled. Quite a few are international students. Most are naturally skeptical, including toward me. Week after week, from their seats around the seminar table, they find ways— both gentle and harsh—to let me know when I have failed to provide clarity or when my arguments are not convincing. Nobody writing a book of this kind could have a better test audience. I wish to dedicate this book to my seminar students at Wellesley. Over the years, many have gone on to careers of their own in the field of food and agriculture to my ever-lasting satisfaction and pride.

FOOD POLITICS

WHAT EVERYONE NEEDS TO KNOW

1

AN OVERVIEW OF FOOD POLITICS

What is food politics?

Since biblical times, government has played a dominant and often a demanding role in food and farming. The book of Genesis (47:24) records that the Egyptian pharaoh took 20 percent of all food production from his farmers as a tax. Some governments in Africa to the present day burden farmers with taxes of comparable magnitude, often collecting the tax indirectly through the price manipulations of state-monopoly marketing agencies or through overvalued currencies that tax the producers of all tradable goods. The goal of such policies is typically to provide the benefit of "cheap food" to urban dwellers, including the employees of the government itself, the army, the police, and the poorly paid civil servants who work, nominally, in the government ministry buildings. These urban dwellers are not as numerous as rural dwellers or as hungry, but they are more literate, better organized, and have the political power to demand such benefits.

In most wealthy countries, by contrast, governments tax urban consumers and provide subsidies to farmers. In these postagricultural societies, farmers are far less numerous than urban dwellers, but they are educated, extremely well organized, and capable of using their political clout to extract resources from the government.

It should not be surprising that the food and farming sectors of all states, ancient and modern, are sites for this kind of political intervention. The authority of the state to collect taxes, provide subsidies, manage exchange rates, and regulate markets presents a political opportunity, and a risk, to both food producers and consumers. Groups within these populations that organize well and take a unified position will be able to capture these powers of the state and then use them to their individual advantage. If they fail to do this, the consequences may be painful when better organized rival organizations succeed.

The struggle over how the losses and gains from state action are allocated in the food and farming sector is what we shall call *food politics*. The distinctive feature is not simply social contestation about food but the potential engagement of state authority. If you and I disagree over the wisdom of eating junk food, that is not food politics. If you and your allies organize and take political action to impose (or to block) new governmental regulations on junk food—for example, keeping certain foods out of public school cafeterias—that is food politics.

Food politics is similar to other kinds of politics in many respects. In democratic societies, it is based on the actions of elected officials inside the state pressured by organized social groups outside government, whereas in authoritarian or one-party states, it emerges from official rulings issued by elites who are autonomous and nonaccountable. Yet food politics is also different from other kinds of politics because of the way food and farming sectors change, as each state struggles to make its own transition from being primarily agricultural and poor to being increasingly industrial and less poor and eventually to being largely postindustrial and wealthy. At each of these stages of development, the power balance between state and society, and between food producers and food consumers, will shift, bringing policy change and a new set of dominant players within the political marketplace.

In the United States and Europe during the peak decades of industrialization in the mid-20th century, it was paradoxically farmers who took the strongest action in the political marketplace for food policy. They felt they were falling behind urban workers in the economic marketplace, so they organized to demand generous subsidies from the state, and they prevailed. Today, as societies in the United States and Europe move into a postindustrial age of much greater urban affluence and many fewer farmers, the policies previously set in place to please and privilege farmers are coming under challenge. The challengers are consumers who want their food to be good as well as cheap, environmentalists who do not like the methods of conventional farming, and also a new generation of farmers promoting less conventional production systems, which are more likely to be small scale, local, and organic.

Society-based food politics of this kind, inside a democratic system, is usually better than the alternative. In authoritarian or one-party states where individuals and groups in society lack the opportunity to take organized political action, serious food policy errors are often made. Famines, for example, are usually confined to nondemocratic countries, such as those living under colonial rule (the Irish potato famine of 1845–52 and the great Indian famine of 1876–78) or the Ukraine famine under Stalin in 1932–33 and, the worst famine of all, the Great Leap Forward famine in China, when an estimated 30 million people died of hunger between 1959–61. The most recent famine tragedy of this second kind occurred when the (badly named) Democratic

People's Republic of Korea imposed fatal food deprivation on millions of powerless citizens in the 1990s.

Is food politics a global or a local phenomenon?

Even in our modern age of globalization, the conduct of food politics remains persistently local. This is because most food is consumed in the same country where it is produced. In many cases, the food is consumed by the same subsistence farmer who produced it. In Africa today, despite globalization, only 15 percent of total cereals consumption is satisfied from imported supplies. In South Asia, only 6 percent of wheat consumption is supplied through imports and only 1 percent of rice consumption. These developing regions are home to hundreds of millions of poor and hungry people, yet because of their poverty, they can afford to purchase very little food from the world market. The heaviest users of world food markets are rich countries, not poor countries; the world's biggest importer of corn is Japan. Typically, rich countries import from other rich countries.

Even some of these rich countries that are heavy importers of some foods and animal feeds, such as Japan, take care not to depend on the world market for basic food staples such as rice. The Japanese government restricts imports of rice to keep foreign supplies out of the domestic market. In the poorest countries as well, national governments jealously guard their authority over staple food markets. In either case, the upper hand usually rests with the nation-state. Intergovernmental organizations (e.g., the World Trade Organization) and multinational food corporations (e.g., Cargill or McDonald's) are typically given only as much room to operate in the marketplace as governments permit.

The politically managed and nonglobalized quality of most food systems is also visible in nutritional outcomes, which diverge dramatically around the world. When it comes to food and agriculture, the world is not flat. The wealthy regions are agriculturally productive and well fed (increasingly, they are overfed), whereas the less wealthy regions are home to farmers not yet highly productive and populations not yet well nourished. In sub-Saharan Africa today, about 60 percent of all citizens are farmers or herders living in the countryside, and one of three is chronically undernourished. In South Asia, roughly 400 million farmers earn less than $1 a day, and approximately 25 percent are malnourished. The needs of these people remain unmet because first the colonizing powers and then their own national governments invested too little in the development of the rural economy. Because of their low political and social status, these farmers have been easy for their "urban-biased" governments to ignore.

In some settings, the politics of food and farming are now addressed globally. For example, agricultural trade restrictions are considered by the World Trade Organization (WTO), and food aid requirements are managed through the UN World Food Programme (WFP). Yet food systems and farming systems remain significantly separate and distinct, divided by ecoregions, levels of industrial development, and cultural traditions. They remain stubbornly under the domination of separate and quite different national governments. As a result, most policy success or failure in the food and farming sectors takes place nationally or locally rather than globally. Thinking globally is generally good advice in sectors like finance or when working on problems such as climate change, but for the politics of food and agriculture, it is often more useful to think nationally or even locally.

Who are the most important actors in food politics?

In the settings where most food politics plays out, a wide range of actors will seek to assert influence, often in conflict with each other. Consumers will want food prices to be low, but farmers will want them to be high. Groups representing these farmers will also struggle among themselves over where the largest government subsidies will go—for example, to producers of imported products versus exported products. (In developing countries, export-oriented farmers usually get more government support, but in rich countries, farmers who compete with imports are usually favored.) At the same time, all these farmers' organizations together will fight to resist tight environmental regulations in league with the industries that supply them with inputs (e.g., manufacturers of fertilizer and pesticides). Food safety and food quality regulations are another divisive problem, setting activist groups who claim to speak for consumers against large food and beverage companies. Retail supermarket chains have separate political interests and objectives as well.

In liberal democratic societies, each of these groups will seek its own special friends inside government. In the United States, organizations that lobby for commercial farmers (known as "farm lobbies") will cultivate members of the agricultural committees of Congress, ensuring that once every 5 years or so these members will draft new legislation (a new "farm bill") to extend the various entitlement programs that provide income subsidies to farmers. To guarantee a majority vote on the floor of both the House and Senate, provisions will be added to please rival groups such as consumers and environmentalists, a standard legislative tactic known as a *committee-based logroll*. Taxpayers are usually the biggest losers when the logs start to roll.

Has the politics of food and agriculture recently been changing?

In today's advanced industrial and postindustrial societies in Europe and North America, the politics of food and agriculture is seeing significant change. There was a time when food consumers in these societies mostly wanted foods that were safe, more convenient to purchase and prepare, and lower in cost. More recently, consumers in these countries have begun to demand other things as well, such as foods with greater freshness and improved nutritional value, foods grown with fewer synthetic chemicals and a smaller carbon footprint, and foods produced with greater attention to the welfare of farm animals. These emerging tastes among increasingly affluent consumers have driven up commercial demand for locally grown foods and for organically grown foods, which are expensive but affordable for high-end consumers.

These shifts have produced conspicuous changes inside the commercial marketplace, and they are now becoming more visible in the political marketplace as well. But here they encounter the entrenched power of lobbyists working on behalf of traditional commercial farming and the industrial food industry. In this new political war over how the nation's food and farming systems should be governed, the battle lines have already been drawn, and the contest is already under way.

2

FOOD PRODUCTION AND POPULATION GROWTH

Who was Thomas Malthus, and why did he see hunger as inevitable?

Thomas Robert Malthus was an English economist who authored in 1798 a highly influential treatise, *An Essay on the Principle of Population*. In this essay, Malthus argued that food production would never stay ahead of population growth because it would be constrained by fixed assets such as land that can only be expanded slowly, while human population tends to grow exponentially. Malthus concluded, "The power of population is so superior to the power of the earth to produce subsistence for man, that premature death must in some shape or other visit the human race." By this, Malthus meant premature death from war, plague, illness, and perhaps even widespread famine.

It was nothing new in 1798 to predict the occurrence of war, plague, and famine, as these had been recurring tragedies in human history. Yet it was entirely new to predict—as Malthus did—that these tragedies were sure to worsen in the future due to the aggregate inability of our Earth to keep pace with human fertility.

Was Malthus right? In 1798 when he wrote his treatise, Earth overall had a population only one-sixth as large as today, so population did increase exponentially just as Malthus foresaw. The frequency of premature death from hunger and famine, however, did not increase. The much larger numbers of people living today tend to live longer and to be far better fed than they were in Malthus's time. In England, specifically, life expectancy at birth has doubled over the past 200 years, from 40 years to more than 80 years. So far, at least, Malthus has been spectacularly wrong.

Yet what about the next 200 years? Earth's population is still increasing, and determined Malthusians insist his prediction may yet come true. Dramatic food production gains over the past two centuries allowed our human population to grow from 1 billion up to 6 billion without any increase in the frequency of premature death, but these gains may not be environmentally sustainable. If we now try to go from a human population of 6 billion up to 9 billion, as is expected by 2050, a Malthusian limit may finally be reached. Until the future reveals itself, a conclusive answer to this question cannot be given.

Was Malthus ever influential?

Malthus was wrong for the first two centuries after he made his prediction, but this did not prevent him from being highly influential, particularly among political elites in England in the 19th century. This in turn led to damaging consequences, particularly in England's colonial territories. Thomas Malthus himself was at one point employed as a professor at the British East India Company training college, and his fatalistic views regarding hunger came to influence England's official policies under the Raj, enabling an indifferent attitude toward the "inevitable" famines that ravaged India during colonial rule. Malthusian thinking also worsened the horrible tragedy of the 1845–49 Irish famine, when a potato blight decimated Ireland's principal food crop. England controlled Ireland at the time, and political elites in London did little to provide relief, in part because they judged the famine to be an inevitable Malthusian consequence of Irish parents producing too many children. It was only because England's political elites embraced Malthusian fatalism, in fact, that the tragic Malthusian prediction came true.

Fortunately, the Malthusian prediction was failing elsewhere at this time because the assumption that food production would remain tightly constrained by the limited land area on Earth proved badly flawed. The land constraint was progressively lifted beginning in the 19th century thanks to the application of modern science to farming. A cascade of new farming technologies developed over the two centuries since Malthus wrote his *Essay*—especially synthetic nitrogen fertilizer and improved seed varieties—allowed crop production on existing farmland to skyrocket. An acre of land today can produce 10 times as much food as it could when Malthus wrote in 1798.

These science-based crop-yield gains were particularly dramatic during the second half of the 20th century. In the United States, average corn yields increased from 34 bushels an acre in the 1940s up to 121 bushels per acre by the 1990s and then up to 156 bushels per acre by 2007. Yields of corn greater than 200 bushels an acre are now common among farmers using the best new seeds and the most sophisticated practices. As farm productivity increased in the 20th century, the price of food declined (the "real" price, discounting for inflation) even though population was steeply rising. The real price of farm commodities paid by consumers fell by more than 50 percent in the United States between 1900 and 2000 despite unprecedented consumption increases driven by high income growth as well as population growth.

Malthus also misjudged long-term trends in human fertility. He assumed birthrates would remain continuously high, thus failing to anticipate the reduction in family size that takes place when societies become wealthier and more urbanized. In urban society, the value of having large families for unskilled farm labor declines, and the payoff from concentrating education investments in fewer children increases. Fertility also tends to fall when more children begin surviving infancy thanks to improved medical practices and even more once education and employment opportunities are extended to young women as well as young men. This always leads to later marriage and hence to fewer years of active childbearing per woman. Because of all these factors in combination, fertility has dropped sharply in all modern industrial societies, and population growth has slowed dramatically.

In some European countries today, population is actually shrinking, and without any premature deaths from war, plague, or famine. In Estonia, the birthrate has recently declined from 2.1 children per woman (the zero-growth replacement rate, or the rate of births necessary to keep the population at a constant number) to only 1.2 children per woman. Rapidly declining fertility is now notable in India as well as in Indonesia, Brazil, and Mexico. These declines in fertility have now reduced the UN projection of Earth's peak population from 12 billion down to just 9 billion, which is only a 50 percent increase from the current level rather than the doubling earlier expected. Malthus has thus been doubly wrong so far. He expected population to increase as rapidly as possible within a constraint of slow food production growth. Instead, we have seen population growth slowing dramatically even in regions where food is more abundant than ever before.

Are Malthusians still influential?

The most recent interlude of acute Malthusian anxiety came in the 1960s and 1970s, at a time of high population growth in Asia, particularly in India and Bangladesh. In 1967, William and Paul Paddock, an agronomist and a former Department of State official, wrote a best seller titled *Famine 1975!* in which they projected India would never be able to feed its growing population. The Paddocks even warned it would be a mistake to give food aid to India because that would keep people alive just long enough to have still more children, leading to even more starvation in the future. Fortunately, this advice was not taken. The U.S. government delivered unprecedented quantities of food aid to India in the 1960s to offset poor harvests, and the larger donor community provided assistance for a significant upgrade in India's own long-term farming potential, an upgrade that came to be known as the green revolution. Improved seeds and fertilizers allowed India's farmers to boost production of wheat and rice dramatically, and by 1975, India was able to terminate food aid completely without a famine.

Paul R. Ehrlich, an American entomologist who originally specialized in butterflies, made a parallel Malthusian argument in a 1968 best seller titled *The Population Bomb*. Ehrlich predicted that hundreds of millions would die in the 1970s due to excessive population growth. He even projected that by 1980 residents in the United States would have a life expectancy of only 42 years. Surprisingly, the book continues to be cited, so perhaps there will always be Malthusians.

Modern Malthusians often look beyond crude population numbers and stress instead the increasing demands for food that will come from growing affluence, leading to increased per capita food consumption. In 1995, for example, Lester R. Brown of the Worldwatch Institute predicted that income growth in China would create a much higher demand for animal products such as meat, eggs, and milk, requiring China to import much more grain from the world market for animal feed. Brown predicted that by 2030 China's need for grain imports would far outstrip the spare production capacity of exporting nations, causing international grain prices to skyrocket. This, he said, would lead to increased hunger in poor importing regions such as Africa, where consumers would not be able to afford the higher prices. When international grain prices finally spiked upward in 2008, Brown tried to claim vindication, but the spike was only temporary and was not caused by Chinese imports. As of 2008, China remained a net exporter of wheat, corn, and rice.

Can we feed a growing population without doing irreversible damage to the environment?

Modern-day Malthusians also add an environmental component to their argument. As we push up food production hoping to keep pace with population and income, too many dry lands or forest lands will be cleared for farming, and too much groundwater or surface water will be used for farm irrigation. Biodiversity will be lost. Food production may increase in the short run, but eventually a combination of falling water tables caused by overpumping, plus desertification caused by the plowing and grazing of dry lands, will push production gains of the past into reverse. This will cause an even more extreme

Malthusian collapse because by then the human population will be even larger. Under this scenario, the most frightening thought is that we may have already exceeded Earth's capacity for *sustainable* food production without realizing it.

Eco-Malthusian "overshoot and collapse" projections of this kind have been in circulation at least since a 1972 report from an organization called the Club of Rome titled *Limits to Growth*. Jared Diamond's 2005 best-selling book titled *Collapse: How Societies Choose to Fail or Succeed* also popularized the overshoot idea. Diamond's account of the disastrous fate of early peoples on Easter Island, Greenland, and the Maya in Central America was intended to drive home the importance of staying within eco-Malthusian limits. The weakness in Diamond's approach was that he could document a vulnerability to overshoot and collapse only among prescientific societies, those lacking the innovation and adjustment potential found in advanced societies today.

Is Africa facing an eco-Malthusian food crisis today?

While the eco-Malthusian vision has not yet been convincing for the world at large, in recent decades it has emerged as a popular way to understand the particular plight of sub-Saharan Africa. In this region, efforts to expand arable land area to boost food production, so as to keep pace with population growth, have led to serious environmental damage in the form of forest loss and habitat destruction. Damage to cropland productivity has been severe as well because population pressures on the land have led to reduced fallow times, hence a more rapid depletion of soil nutrients. This in turn has constrained production. In some African countries, average crop yields per hectare have actually declined, and for sub-Saharan Africa as a whole over the past several decades, total food production per person has declined. On a per capita basis since 1980, the production of maize (Africa's most important food crop, a staple food to 300 million people) has fallen by 14 percent. Hunger simultaneously has increased. The number of Africans who are "food insecure"—those consuming less than the nutritional target of 2,100 calories per day—increased from 300 million in 1992 to roughly 450 million by 2006. One of every three Africans is now chronically undernourished, and the U.S. Department of Agriculture projects that under a business-as-usual scenario, the number of undernourished people in Africa will increase another 30 percent by 2020 to reach 645 million. In Africa, the pessimistic eco-Malthusian prediction might seem to be coming true.

Africa's problems are tragic and severe, yet they do not take the form of a classic Malthusian trap, where population growth outstrips food production potential. This is because food production in Africa today is far less than the known potential for the region. African farmers today use almost no fertilizer (only one-tenth as much as farmers in Europe use), only 4 percent of their cropland has been irrigated, and most of the cropped area in Africa is not planted with seeds improved through scientific plant breeding. As a consequence, average cereal crop yields per hectare in Africa are only about one-fifth as high as in the developed world. Africa is failing to keep up with population growth not because it has exhausted its potential but instead because too little has been invested in developing that potential. Typically in Africa today, governments spend only about 5 percent of their budget on any kind of agricultural investments, even though 60 percent of their citizens depend on the farming sector for income and employment.

If food production fails to keep up because nobody invests to make farms more productive, that should be seen as an acute public policy crisis but not exactly a vindication of Malthus.

Do Malthusians try to reduce population growth?

Thomas Malthus, in his day, never put much stock in efforts to control fertility. By the 20th century, however, public and private interventions to encourage "family planning" were commonplace in the industrial world. Births per woman were rapidly declining there anyway, so it became more common for modern-day Malthusians to advocate similar interventions to bring down fertility in developing countries. Some even suggested that such interventions should go beyond voluntary measures. In 1975, Lester Brown argued that the United States and Canada, then the world's leading grain exporters, should ration their sales in times of tight supply only to foreign customers who were doing something about their own population growth. Brown said it was the responsibility of the "North American Breadbasket" to use its powerful control over food exports to push developing countries toward tougher measures on population control.

Advocacy of this kind fell out of favor later in the 1970s, after China's coercive one-child family policy led to female infants being killed by parents who wanted their one child to be a son and when a state-sponsored sterilization policy in India led to explosive social tensions between Hindus and Muslims. In the decade between the 1974 World Population Conference in Bucharest and the 1984 International Conference on Population in Mexico City, fashion in the international assistance community shifted from rigid "supply-side" efforts to bring down fertility (e.g., giving men and women access to modern contraception) to a new "demand-side" approach that focused on reducing the desire for more children. This demand-side approach was advanced through an emphasis on income growth, increased child survival, and a promotion of education and employment opportunities for girls and young women that would forestall immediate marriage and childbearing.

Aggressive supply-side efforts to limit fertility also came under attack from the Christian Right in America in the 1980s as one part of a campaign against the 1973 *Roe v. Wade* Supreme Court decision that decriminalized abortion. Abortion opponents did not have the means to get their way inside the United States, but they did manage, beginning under the presidency of Ronald Reagan, to place tighter restrictions on the use of American foreign assistance for family planning purposes. Mindful that aggressive supply-side efforts at fertility control were no longer acceptable either to the political Left or the political Right, most Malthusians retreated to fatalistic pessimism, in the style of their original namesake.

Do Malthusians argue we should reduce food consumption?

For Malthusians who no longer wish to advocate fertility control, the alternative is a call for reduced food consumption per capita. In 1971, a young countercultural food activist named Frances Moore Lappe wrote a widely influential book (3 million copies sold) titled *Diet for a Small Planet*, which argued that meat consumption in rich countries implied using up scarce land resources to grow grain to feed chickens, pigs, and cattle, when the grain should instead be used to prevent starvation in poor countries. Lappe argued against beef consumption in particular, observing that the protein beef cattle consumed in feed was 21 times greater than what they finally made available in their meat for human consumption. In a world of tightening food supply, perhaps the only escape would be a move toward vegetarian diets.

The idea that reducing meat consumption in rich countries can help hungry people in poor countries has ethical appeal but only limited practical effect. If beef consumption in rich countries declined, commercial demand for animal feed would decline as well, resulting in less grain being produced. In a market economy, if commercial demand for grain goes away, grain production goes away. Even if grain production did not fall, nobody would wish to take on the enormous expense of shipping the surplus in large volume to reach hungry people living in the remote countryside of poor countries. Also, in today's rich countries, it would be good for public health if less meat were consumed, but in much of Africa, becoming a vegetarian is not an option. On many dry lands in Africa, there is not enough rainfall to grow cereal crops, so the only source of food is grass-fed animals, such as goats and cattle.

Beyond personal health, the best reason for people in rich countries to eat less meat is to relieve the pollution burden large livestock herds have come to place on the atmosphere. Dietary demand for livestock products—meat, milk, and eggs—has driven a steady increase in the earth's population of animals (cattle, pigs, chickens, goats, and sheep) raised for food. The feeding and processing of these animals make large demands on land and energy, generating greenhouse gases. In 2006, the Food and Agriculture Organization of the United Nations (FAO) released a report titled *Livestock's Long Shadow* showing that livestock are now responsible for 18 percent of all greenhouse gas emissions, a bigger share than for transport.

Carbon emissions come from the cutting of forests for pasture, the planting of crops for animal feed, the cultivation of those feed crops, the production of fertilizer for those crops, and the transport of livestock products. Potent greenhouse gases such as methane and nitrous oxide also come from the digestive systems of ruminant animals and from animal manure. Soon after this FAO report appeared, an organization named People for the Ethical Treatment of Animals (PETA) chided ex-Vice President Al Gore for never mentioning dietary changes as one of the ways people might help contain the risks of global warming.

3

THE POLITICS OF HIGH FOOD PRICES

Do high food prices mean we face a food crisis?

On two recent occasions—the first in 1973–74 and then once again in 2007–08—the price of internationally traded food commodities jumped upward sharply, interrupting a century-long pattern of real price decline. On both occasions, political commentators concluded that the world was facing a *food crisis*.

International food price fluctuations are easily misinterpreted. The underlying causes often originate from beyond the food and farm sector, and the resulting impacts on actual human hunger are usually limited because use of the international market is limited. Most governments around the world limit and manage their food imports for the purpose of stabilizing domestic prices, presumably to the benefit of their own farmers when international prices fall and to the benefit of their own consumers when prices rise. When multiple governments do this at the same time, price instability is exported into the international marketplace. In international markets, the price of wheat, corn, or rice is consequently quite volatile, but most consumers pay the stabilized domestic price, not the destabilized international price.

The psychology of panic also plays a role. When importers notice a rising price trend in the international market, some will accelerate the timing of their purchases to be safe in case the price does go higher. When they all do this at the same time, international prices rise more quickly. At this point, the governments of some exporting countries will begin to worry that international demand could push up prices in their own domestic markets, so they begin imposing restrictions on exports. When all the exporting countries do this at the same time, the international price rises in an even steeper spike. This further panics importers, who fear they will not be able to purchase what they need unless they buy immediately. This leads to even more demand pressure on the limited quantities of food still available for export, and the rise in international prices becomes nearly vertical. At the peak of the spike, stories appear in the media about bad weather, failing harvests, and dwindling food stocks, making the panic worse and briefly driving international prices to absurd levels. Inside most domestic economies, however, the price of food can remain surprisingly stable.

The world does face a serious food crisis, but the best way to judge the magnitude of the crisis is to measure actual hunger rather than price fluctuations on the world market. This is because most of the world's genuinely hungry people do not get their food from the world market. As will be explained in the next chapter, chronic undernutrition currently afflicts more than 800 million individuals around the world whether international food prices are high or low. Most of these people live in the impoverished countryside in South Asia and sub-Saharan Africa. They are significantly cut off from world markets by their physical distance from coastal import terminals and by poor rural road systems that create exceptionally high transport costs. These people are hungry because their own productivity and income are low, not because prices on the world market are high. Most users of international food markets are well-fed consumers in rich countries, not the hungry rural poor in developing countries.

Sudden spikes in international food prices do cause hardships for poor populations in some developing countries significantly dependent on food imports from the world market, especially in the Caribbean, Central America, and West Africa, yet these temporary and geographically restricted hardships are not the same as a systemic world food crisis. International food price spikes do not cause famines (famines are of local origin, as will be shown in chapter 5), nor are they the leading cause of chronic undernutrition. They are nonetheless dramatic events that are costly to many and undeniably dangerous for some.

Why did food prices rise in 2008?

The price of most food commodities available for export spiked up sharply in 2007–08. By April 2008, the export price of corn (maize) had doubled over the previous 2 years, rice prices had tripled in just 3 months, and wheat available for export had reached its highest price in 28 years. The *New York Times*, in a lead editorial, declared this a "World Food Crisis." In some poor countries heavily dependent on imports, urban populations took to the streets in protest. Demonstrations and rioting took place in Egypt, Cameroon, Ivory Coast, Senegal, and Ethiopia. In Haiti, the prime minister was forced to resign after a week of street violence over the price of rice and beans. In Pakistan and Thailand, army troops were deployed to deter food theft from fields and warehouses. The president of the

World Bank, Robert Zoellick, warned that high food prices were particularly dangerous in poor countries where the purchase of food requires half to three-quarters of a person's income. "There is no margin for survival," he said.

The 2008 price spike lasted through early summer, and parallel spikes in fertilizer and fuel prices worsened the crisis by making crops too expensive to plant and by diverting corn to produce biofuels as a substitute for gasoline. By late summer, all three of these panic-driven price bubbles—for food, fertilizer, and fuel—had reached their peak and began to deflate. A global financial panic in September 2008 then reversed expectations of continued global economic growth, turning the commodity price decline into a full collapse. International crude oil prices fell in just a few months from $142 a barrel all the way down to only $40 a barrel. In international food markets, export prices fell by 40 percent or more. International food prices did not fall all the way down to where they had been before the spike began because a number of countries, including China, were buying heavily to rebuild their food stocks just in case international prices began rising again.

From inside the food and farming sector, the single biggest source of this dramatic price spike had been changes in trade policy. Once commodity prices began moving upward, a number of countries decided to place restrictions on food exports so as to protect their consumers from price inflation at home. China imposed export taxes on grains and grain products. Argentina raised export taxes on wheat, corn, and soybeans. Russia raised export taxes on wheat. Malaysia and Indonesia imposed export taxes on palm oil. Egypt, Cambodia, Vietnam, and Indonesia eventually banned exports of rice. India, the world's third largest rice exporter, banned exports of rice other than basmati. These national trade restrictions, imposed all at the same time, created a sudden shortage of food available for export on the world market, driving international prices much higher and deepening the panic buying. As media reports of shortages proliferated, panic buying even spread to the United States, where frightened consumers began descending on stores to buy rice. In April 2008, Costco Wholesale Corporation and Wal-Mart's Sam's Club had to limit sales of rice to four bags per customer per visit.

At a deeper level, the food price spike reflected macroeconomic forces from beyond the food and farming sector. Market bubbles for real estate and equities had burst in 2007, leaving investors with nowhere to put their money, so some chose commodities funds, an investment move that drove up the price of commodities futures and helped feed the psychology of commodity shortage and the bubble in food prices. The economywide nature of this phenomenon was reflected in the fact that nearly all commodities prices spiked upward in 2008, not only food. In fact, petroleum, metals, and fertilizer prices spiked higher than food.

The 2008 price spike in international food markets did not result from diminished food production. In rice markets, for example, export prices tripled in 2008 even though world production continued to increase more rapidly than world consumption. There was a shortage of rice available in international markets due to temporary export restrictions, but there was not a shortage of rice overall. Fortunately, only about 5 percent of global rice consumption is satisfied through world trade, so the high export prices of 2008 had severely damaging effects on only limited numbers of consumers worldwide.

In any given year, bad weather will cause food production in some countries to decline, and 2007 was no exception.

Ukraine and Russia experienced a second year in a row of drought, and Australia experienced a third year in a row. These events were cited by some as reasons for the increase in world wheat prices, but the panic in world markets was driven more by Russian and Argentine export restrictions on wheat than by any global shortage overall. In 2007, global stocks of wheat were lower relative to consumption than they had been for a number of years, but this reflected conscious decisions in major countries to carry smaller stocks so as to save money, not faltering production. The fact that stocks were low contributed to the intensity of the panic, but low stocks did not cause the panic. Nor was high food consumption in China the source of the problem. Rapid income growth was driving up China's demand for food, but Chinese production was also increasing, and in 2007–08, when international prices were spiking, China was actually a net exporter of rice, wheat, and corn.

Did an increased use of food as biofuel cause the crisis?

A more plausible demand-side explanation for the price spike in 2008 was the increased use of agricultural commodities in that year for biofuels, such as ethanol produced from corn. In 2007, Congress had passed an Energy Independence and Security Act that mandated a use of 36 billion gallons of renewable fuel in the United States by 2022, with up to 15 billion gallons of that to come from corn. This new official mandate, when added to rising fuel prices on the world market since 2005, triggered a wave of investments in ethanol production that nearly tripled production capacity in just 4 years' time, up to about 12 billion gallons, diverting increased quantities of corn away from food use and into fuel. The share of U.S. corn production used to produce ethanol increased from 10 percent in 2003 to 24 percent by 2008. In fact, 70 percent of all increased corn production globally between 2004 and 2007 was diverted to biofuel use, and this was clearly a contributing factor to higher corn prices in 2008. Europe had a biofuels promotion policy as well, and by 2008, half of all rapeseed production in Europe was being diverted to the production of biodiesel transport fuels.

Yet even this biofuels factor must be kept in perspective. As demand for biofuel crops increased, total supply increased as well, diminishing any trade-off between fuel and food. The share of the world's agricultural land diverted to biofuel production thus remains small—only 5 percent in the United States and less than 4 percent in the other top five biofuels-producing countries. If biofuels demand had been the leading driver in the 2008 food price spike, corn prices would have risen more sharply than wheat or rice, yet corn rose less sharply than either.

The expansion of biofuels production in 2007–08 did reveal an important link between food prices and energy prices. When energy prices go up, more food is diverted to biofuels use, and production of food becomes more costly due to higher diesel fuel and fertilizer prices. Because of such linkages, every 100 percent increase in the price of petroleum today results in roughly a 20 percent increase in the price of grain. On the other hand, when oil prices fell sharply later in 2008, grain prices also fell, and the need to use corn for ethanol declined. By 2009, many ethanol plants built in haste in 2007 were standing idle or operating well below capacity.

Did people go hungry when prices went up?

People were hurt economically by the price spike of 2008, and some were even temporarily pushed back into poverty and undernutrition, but in most cases the income squeeze did not bring a rise in hunger. Protests broke out among urban populations in some countries where food imports had satisfied a large share of the diet before 2008, but urban populations in poor countries are generally less hungry than rural populations. In Cairo, for example, there were bread riots in April 2008 in which two people died, but bread in Egypt is normally so cheap in urban areas (the government controls the market to keep it that way) that obesity is now a more serious health problem than hunger. The citizens of Cairo saw their disposable income shrink when the price of bread went up, so they rioted, but few suffered from actual hunger. Food price riots are not unusual in urban centers in the developing world. In both Africa and Latin America in the 1980s, urban riots took place in a number of countries when governments terminated subsidies designed to keep food artificially cheap. The subsidies were terminated to satisfy conditions then being imposed by the International Monetary Fund (IMF) in return for access to stabilization loans during a world debt crisis at the time, so the resulting riots were facetiously dubbed "IMF riots."

Estimates vary as to the number of people who temporarily went hungry due to the international price spike of 2008. At the time, the World Bank produced a provisional estimate that 100 million people around the world had been pushed into poverty because of the higher food prices, thus becoming more vulnerable to hunger. This estimate was based on a computer model of food markets rather than the collection of any new food consumption data, and the computer model made several dubious assumptions, including one that trade policies would not change as food prices went up. In fact, changes in food trade policies had been a leading cause of the crisis, as noted earlier.

Even if we accept the estimate that an additional 100 million people became poor and hungry in 2008 due to the price spike, the magnitude of this temporary hunger is still only one-eighth the magnitude of the persistent hunger around the world that is caused by deep poverty. Roughly 800 million people around the world were chronically malnourished due to poverty even before the 2008 price crisis began. In sub-Saharan Africa in 2005, a year when food was cheap on the world market, people in 23 of 37 countries in that region were consuming less than their nutritional requirements, and one-third of all citizens were undernourished. Even if international food prices eventually fall all the way back down to this low 2005 level, this larger pattern of persistent hunger will still be there.

Had anything like the 2008 price spike happened before?

The 2008 food price spike was in many ways similar to an event that occurred in the 1970s. Between 1971 and 1974, the price of wheat and corn on the world market more than doubled, and the price of soybeans rose so high that even the United States briefly imposed an export ban. In November 1974, *Time* magazine branded this a "world food crisis," asserting that hunger and famine were ravaging "hundreds of millions of the poorest citizens in at least 40 nations."

This earlier food price spike exhibited a number of characteristics similar to the spike of 2008. Then, just as in 2008, the price of all commodities, not only food, was spiking upward. The macroeconomic explanation on that occasion was inflationary growth linked to lax monetary policies by the Federal Reserve Board in the United States. (In 2008 as well, the Federal Reserve Board was cutting interest rates to record low levels.) Also, just as in 2008, the spike in international food prices was made worse by trade restrictions. In addition to a temporary U.S. embargo on soybean sales, Argentina, Brazil, Thailand, Myanmar (then Burma), and the European Union (then the Common Market) restricted food exports, stabilizing prices at home but destabilizing international market prices. Also in the 1970s, just as in 2008, food riots broke out in urban neighborhoods. As in 2008, the UN Food and Agriculture Organization (FAO) hosted a global conference in Rome to address the crisis. At this FAO conference in 1974, U.S. Secretary of State Henry Kissinger called for action to ensure that within 10 years no child should have to go to bed hungry. Parallel calls to action were heard at the 2008 FAO conference. The danger is that these policy responses to long-term hunger will be put on the shelf once international food prices come back down, which is exactly what happened after the 1974 panic subsided.

The price spike of 1974 was brought to an end by a slowdown in economic growth worldwide, particularly following a second major oil price shock in 1979 and then a tightening of U.S. interest rate policies. By 1981, the American economy had slumped into a recession, and real economic growth rates outside the United States fell to 1.6 percent. In Latin America between 1981 and 1983, economic growth rates actually turned negative. In this altered macroeconomic environment, international food prices dropped, and an erroneous conclusion was drawn that the world food crisis was finally over. The price spike of 2008 was reversed in a similar fashion, as a result of the 2008–09 global financial crisis and subsequent world recession. By mid-2009, the World Bank was projecting a 4.5 percent contraction in the economic output of the world's richest countries and a 2.9 percent contraction overall. Further, they projected economic growth rates in the developing world to fall to 1.2 percent in 2009, a severe drop from the 8.1 percent pace set in 2007. It was this broad contraction of economic growth that brought international food prices down from the 2008 peak, not a sudden increase in the supply of food available.

Subsequent analysis of the earlier price spike from the 1970s teaches an important lesson about international food prices and hunger. In this earlier episode, more people went hungry *after* the international price of food fell, during the economic recession years that followed. In fact, it was only when the publicly declared food crisis ended in the 1980s that the real food crisis began. Data on food consumption from the FAO reveal that between 1971 and 1974, when international food prices were high, consumption of cereals increased on a per capita basis in most poor countries because so many domestic markets were insulated from international price fluctuations and because economic growth ensured people had more income to spend on food. It was not until the decade of the 1980s, when international food prices were low again, that food consumption trends in Latin America and in Africa worsened due to the slowdown in income growth. If there should be a parallel period of much lower economic growth in the developing world after 2009, caused by smaller net flows of private capital to poor countries following the economic slump in rich countries, food consumption trends will again worsen, and a real food crisis will deepen just as the crisis in world food prices is declared over.

When international food prices spike upward, consumption adjustments are made, but most are made in rich countries rather than poor countries because the rich are the heaviest users of these international markets. In international corn markets, for example, the biggest importer is Japan, and the biggest exporter is the United States, so when international corn prices go up, these countries make the biggest adjustments. Typically, the first adjustment will be to feed less corn to farm animals such as chickens, pigs, and cattle. In wealthy countries, the fact that a great deal of grain is fed to animals provides a buffer against price fluctuations for food. In 1974, when corn prices more than doubled, the United States reduced the feeding of grain to livestock by 25 percent, which freed up more grain for direct consumption as food. Herd sizes declined, which eventually led to higher meat prices and reduced meat consumption, but in wealthy societies, where overnutrition and obesity are growing public health problems, this is not entirely a bad outcome.

4

THE POLITICS OF
CHRONIC HUNGER

How do we define and measure hunger?

We all feel momentary hunger just before most meals. If these meals are inadequate, we eventually experience chronic undernutrition in the form of either a calorie deficit or a micronutrient deficit. A calorie deficit occurs when intake of energy is lower than what the body burns. A micronutrient deficit is not having enough minerals and vitamins, such as iron, zinc, iodine, or vitamin A. Typical cases of undernutrition feature both calorie and micronutrient deficits at the same time.

Chronic undernutrition is most precisely measured one person at a time, or one child at a time, because most of the world's undernutrition is suffered by children younger than 3 years. Inadequate early nutrition from conception to age 2 can lead to reduced cognition and increased susceptibility to infectious disease. Undernutrition is a leading cause of infant mortality. Children under 5 die four times as often in underfed Africa as in today's rich countries.

It is relatively easy for clinicians to measure some kinds of individual caloric energy deficits. If a child's stature is too short relative to his or her age, clinicians conclude the child suffers from *stunting*. If a child's weight is too low relative to his or her stature, the child suffers from *wasting*. An unusually short and skinny child suffers from stunting and wasting at the same time.

Human stature can be affected by genetics as well as nutrition, so if an individual is genetically disposed to be short, small stature may not reflect ill health. This is known as the "small but healthy" effect. If, however, a large population has a below-average stature, long-term effects on health are statistically known to be adverse. Compared to a century ago, the average adult male in the United States today is 3 inches taller and also has a much longer life expectancy.

Traditional measures of undernutrition based on calorie requirements contain greater ambiguities. Since 1985, experts from the FAO and the World Health Organization (WHO) have recommended an average energy intake of 2,250 calories a day to sustain light activity, but even among adults, levels of activity vary dramatically both across and within societies. The methods for measuring calorie intake are also a problem. The FAO attempts to measure food-energy deficits through surveys of sample households, but this assumes that families report their recent food intake accurately, and it ignores unequal food distribution within households. An even less reliable FAO technique for calculating calorie intake is the "national food balance" approach, based on the total food production of a nation, plus food stocks, plus imports, minus food exports, divided by total population. This method falls short because it lumps foods of different nutritional value into a single category, and it fails to capture the unequal food consumption patterns that prevail within countries.

All of these approaches tend as well to miss micronutrient deficiencies, referred to as *hidden hunger*. Lack of iron is the most widespread nutrition deficit in the world, yet it easily escapes direct notice. According to the World Health Organization, 42 percent of pregnant women worldwide suffer from anemia (a risk factor for hemorrhage and death in childbirth), and in many African countries, four of five children under 5 years do not get enough iron.

Observational problems such as these have inspired efforts to build malnutrition measures more closely tied to actual health outcomes. For example, the International Food Policy Research Institute (IFPRI) in Washington, D.C., has developed a Global Hunger Index (GHI) for measuring undernutrition in developing countries based on three equally weighted indicators. The first indicator is an FAO calculation of the share of the national population estimated to be energy deficient in terms of calorie intake. The second indicator is a WHO calculation of the prevalence of wasting or stunting among children under age 5. The third indicator is rates of child mortality (admittedly, this third indicator mixes damage from inadequate diet with damage from lack of medical care or from various unhealthy factors in the environment). Combining these three equally weighted components, the GHI then ranks developing countries on a 100-point scale, with zero being the best (no hunger) and 100 being the worst (no country reaches this worst extreme). To help interpret the national scores, IFPRI states that a score greater than 10 indicates a serious problem, a score greater than 20 is alarming, and a score greater than 30 is extremely alarming.

How many people are chronically malnourished, and where can they be found?

When chronic malnutrition is measured using FAO's single food-energy deficit indicator, an up-to-date count of total numbers of hungry people worldwide can be generated year by year. Of course, since global population is still increasing, a growing hunger count does not necessarily mean higher hunger prevalence. For the period 2003–05, FAO estimated there were 848 million undernourished people worldwide, 98 percent living in the developing world, and 62 percent living in either South Asia (313 million) or sub-Saharan Africa (212 million). In 2007, FAO increased this total number to 923 million, and then in December 2008, taking the world food crisis into account, up to 963 million. Finally, in the spring of 2009, taking the onset of a world recession into account, FAO increased its count of undernourished people to a total of 1,020 million. Between 2005 and 2009, the numbers of undernourished people in sub-Saharan Africa increased by 53 million.

IFPRI's Global Hunger Index measures the severity and prevalence of undernutrition but not in absolute numbers; still, the regional hot spots are the same. In the 2008 GHI, which was based on 2006 data, sub-Saharan Africa had a regionwide score of 23.3 (in the alarming range), and South Asia had a score of 23.0 (also alarming). Looking at the separate components of the index, the major problem in South Asia was the high prevalence of underweight and stunted children younger than 5 years. In Africa, the high GHI was driven primarily by high child mortality. The countries with the most worrisome GHI scores were predominately in sub-Saharan Africa, led by the Democratic Republic of Congo, Eritrea, Burundi, Niger, and Sierra Leone. War and violent conflict were factors in several of these countries.

When GHI scores for 2008 are compared to scores for 1990, some trends become clear. The regional GHI score in South Asia fell from 34 to 23, still much too high but a significant

improvement. In Southeast Asia, the GHI score fell from
14 to 9, and in Latin America, from 9 to 6, as these two regions
continued to move farther away from anything that could be
called a pervasive hunger crisis. In sub-Saharan Africa, there
was some modest regionwide improvement as well, from a
GHI score of 26 to 23.3, but in 10 individual African countries,
the GHI measure of hunger prevalence increased, including
by 17 percent in poorly governed Zimbabwe and by a tragic
57 percent in the war-torn Democratic Republic of Congo.

Africa's distinct problems with hunger are also highlighted
through measures of underweight children (the wasting
measure) 5 years or younger. In Asia, nearly half of all children (45.4 percent) were considered underweight in 1980, but
that share fell to 24.8 percent by 2005. In Latin America and
the Caribbean, the share of underweight children fell over
the same time period from 12.5 percent to 5.5 percent. But in
Africa, the share of underweight children actually increased
slightly between 1980 and 2005 from 23.5 percent to 24.5
percent. Because total population in Africa doubled during
this same time period, the total number of underweight children doubled as well.

Which groups of people suffer most from chronic undernutrition?

In the developing world, chronic undernutrition tends to
concentrate among specific populations. Preschool children
are most at risk, but among the poor, adults suffer as well,
particularly pregnant and nursing women. Household surveys
in Burundi, Ghana, Kenya, and Malawi show that more than
90 percent of those who were poor (living on less than $1 a
day) were also hungry, with a diet either lacking in diversity
or a daily energy intake below 2,200 calories. In Bangladesh,

74 percent of those who were poor were also hungry. People who live in remote rural areas are also likelier to be hungry compared with those living in cities or close to roads and rail lines. In addition, those with fewer years of schooling are likelier to be hungry, and in Asia, those who do not own land are likelier to be hungry. Ethnic minorities are likelier to be hungry. In Central America, for example, stunting is more than twice as widespread among indigenous children compared to nonindigenous children. In South Asia, hill tribes and members of so-called scheduled castes suffer greater nutrition deficits than others. In Sri Lanka, Indian Tamils are at a disadvantage. In Africa, female-headed households are more at risk. Yet in all poor countries, it is children, especially orphans and street children, who tend to be the most deprived.

Urban poverty is pervasive in much of the developing world, yet it is rural dwellers who are likelier to be hungry. There are roughly twice as many poor and hungry people in the African countryside as there are in urban areas. In South Asia, there are roughly three times as many poor and hungry people in the countryside as in urban areas. Paradoxically and perversely, a majority of all these poor and hungry people in the developing world are farmers or pastoralists—people engaged in producing food. It is the low productivity of farming and animal grazing among the rural poor that is the chief cause of their chronic poverty, and it is their poverty that is the chief cause of their undernutrition.

How is poverty measured?

Measuring poverty is not easy in subsistence economies where few of life's needs are bought and sold. In these cases, measures of consumption are frequently used as a proxy for income. Household expenditure surveys generate measures of the value of per capita consumption, and these figures are then translated into dollars using exchange rates adjusted for local differences in the purchasing power of currency. Those with expenditures below $1 a day are understood to be poor. Using this approach, the International Food Policy Research Institute calculates that there were 969 million poor people in the developing world in 2004, with 47 percent living in South Asia and 31 percent in sub-Saharan Africa.

Despite continued population growth, both the prevalence and the incidence of this kind of poverty have been decreasing in most of the developing world, an achievement that deserves more frequent celebration. Between 1990 and 2004, the number of poor people in the developing world as a whole fell by 23 percent, from 1,248 million to 969 million. The number of poor in East Asia and the Pacific actually fell by 64 percent, from 476 million to 169 million. Despite high population growth, the total number of poor people in South Asia also fell, from 479 million to 446 million. Only in sub-Saharan Africa did numbers of poor people increase, from 241 million to 298 million. This increase resulted from income growth too slow to stay ahead of continued population growth.

Poverty results in malnutrition because the poor lack the means to purchase a sufficient quantity and variety of food. For the poor living on less than $1 a day in Africa, the share of the household budget that must be devoted to food is typically more than 70 percent. In South Asia, it is typically more than 60 percent. The rest goes to other necessities such as clothing, fuel, and housing. Basic food expenditure requirements thus leave little or nothing for household investments in improved health or enhanced education outcomes for children, so the children often remain poor as well, perpetuating the cycle.

Chronic hunger also afflicts many who live on more than $1 a day. In Kenya and Senegal, 60 percent of all hungry people actually live on more than $1 a day; in Pakistan, this number is 80 percent, and in Guatemala, it's 90 percent.

What are the political consequences of chronic undernutrition?

Chronic undernutrition seldom triggers political change. This is because poor and hungry communities usually lack organized political voice. They are too often confined to remote regions in the countryside, cut off from political affairs by their physical distance from the capital city and their lack of access to roads and the electronic media. Many of these poor and hungry people are also illiterate, further reducing their capacity to organize for political action. Many are poor women who are busy all day raising their children and caring for the elderly, with little time left over to become involved in politics. Also, society may not permit them to play a political role if they are women, from a disadvantaged caste, or from a marginalized racial or ethnic group. Finally, many live in countries governed by regimes that monopolize power within a single ruling party, a single dynastic family, the military, or a theocracy of religious clerics. For political systems such as these, poor and hungry people in the countryside are easy to ignore.

It is mostly the nonhungry and the nonpoor that pose threats to governing authorities. When food prices increase, urban populations that may be at little risk of hunger can nonetheless take to the streets to protest the squeeze on their income. In Egypt in 2008, there were riots in Cairo caused by shortages of government-subsidized bread due to much higher import costs for wheat, but few in Cairo were actually going hungry. Bread prices had been so heavily subsidized for urban dwellers in Egypt over the years that average per capita calorie consumption was roughly comparable to European standards. Health problems linked to obesity are now more of a problem in Egypt than those linked to undernutrition. It is telling that none of the food protests of 2008 broke out in a country for which IFPRI had calculated a GHI in the highest category of extremely alarming. The weak political voice of the rural poor, even while they suffer from alarming hunger, helps explain why the hunger is allowed to persist for so long.

Is chronic undernutrition a problem in the United States?

America's current health crisis from food is linked far more to overnutrition than to undernutrition. Just one century ago, hunger was still widespread because average consumer income in the United States was only one-fourth as high as it is today, and farm commodity prices at that time were twice as high. This food system of the past is nothing we should wish to re-create. At the beginning of the 20th century, the average American spent 41 percent of personal income on food (compared to just 12 percent today), and low-income Americans often could not afford a healthy diet. During the hard times of the Great Depression in the 1930s, several thousand Americans died each year from diseases such as pellagra (niacin deficiency), beri-beri (thiamine deficiency), rickets (vitamin D deficiency), and scurvy (vitamin C deficiency). In 1938, more than 20 percent of preschool children in America had rickets, with hundreds dying from this debilitating ailment.

During the second half of the 20th century, these problems were largely overcome thanks to reduced poverty plus a continued decline in food commodity prices. Public policy interventions also played an important role. A National School Lunch Act was passed by Congress in 1946, partly in reaction to the poor nutritional status discovered among young men drafted into service in World War II. Then in the 1960s, media reports of scandalous poverty and hunger in Appalachia prompted the dramatic expansion of a federal Food Stamp program designed to help low-income families purchase a nutritionally adequate diet. In the 1970s, a Special Supplemental Nutrition Program for Women, Infants, and Children (the WIC program) was created to improve the health of low-income pregnant women, new mothers, infants, and young children at nutritional risk.

These programs produced gratifying results. When a team of physicians restudied conditions in poor regions in America in 1977, they noticed a dramatic change: "Our first and overwhelming impression is that there are far fewer grossly malnourished people in this country today than there were ten years ago.... The Food Stamp Program, the nutritional components of Head Start, school lunch and breakfast programs, and ... [WIC] have made the difference."

Food assistance programs are costly for taxpayers. The total federal food and nutrition program budget in 2006 was $53 billion, considerably more than the budget cost of subsidies to farmers that year. The Food Stamp program is the single largest component of America's food assistance budget, with 28 million people enrolled as of 2008. The average recipient family has a gross monthly income of less than $700, and roughly half of all participants in the program are children, with 61 percent living in single-parent households. The average household participating now receives an electronic debit card that can be used to purchase about $215 worth of food each month. Among all recipients, 43 percent are white, 33 percent African American, and 19 percent Hispanic.

Not all food purchases made through this program are additional to purchases that would have been made anyway; to a significant extent, poor households use the stamps to cover their normal food purchases, which allows them to allocate greater funds to other things such as housing, clothing, health, and education. The Food Stamp program also functions as income insurance for people temporarily laid off from work. Most Food Stamp participants receive benefits for less than a year, and the median length of participation in the program is only 6 to 8 months. If this important Food Stamp program had been given a more accurate name—"an income supplement and insurance program for the poor"—it would enjoy far less political support in Congress. It gains strong bipartisan support because of its brand as a program against hunger. It also enjoys broad political support because it is routinely bundled into the same legislative package that delivers subsidies to farmers, the so-called farm bill, ensuring that representatives from agricultural districts will vote for food stamps in return for urban votes to preserve farm subsidies.

As America's hunger crisis came to be supplanted by an obesity crisis, the Food Stamp program was forced to adjust. In 2008, the Food and Nutrition Service of the Department of Agriculture began calling the program the Supplemental Nutrition Assistance Program (SNAP) in an attempt to underscore a new emphasis on educating recipients to pick healthy foods. Efforts have also been made to provide more card-reading terminals at farmers' markets to make it easier for food stamp recipients to purchase local fresh produce. There is little evidence, however, that the original Food Stamp program worsened obesity among the poor. Comparisons between the poor populations in America that choose to receive food stamps and those that do not (it is a voluntary program) reveal no differences in the likelihood of an overweight or obese body mass index (BMI) for men and children and only a small propensity for unhealthy weight gain among the adult women who participate.

In America today, areas of poverty persist but with greatly diminished effects on nutrition. Average consumption of protein, vitamins, and minerals is virtually identical for poor versus middle-class children, and average calorie consumption is comparably excessive for both groups. Most poor children in America today grow to be, on average, 1 inch taller and 10 pounds heavier than the GIs who stormed the beaches of Normandy in World War II, and official measures of hunger confirm these gains. The federal government's standard for measuring chronic hunger is an inability, on an average given day, for one or more household members to afford enough food. Using this standard, chronic hunger is now experienced by only 0.5 percent of American households. Social and political mobilization around hunger issues is still visible in America (church donations, local food banks, local walks for hunger), and in times of economic downturn these programs bring tangible economic benefit to the disadvantaged, but the nation's problems with chronic hunger have largely been overcome.

What policy remedies are available in developing countries?

Poor countries with large numbers of undernourished people cannot afford expensive entitlement programs similar to Food Stamps because there are too many people in need relative to the limited budget resources and institutional capacity available. Many governments have tried to maintain systems to subsidize food purchase in urban areas either through government-funded "fair price shops," where citizens holding ration cards can purchase cheap bread or flour, or by flooding urban markets with government-purchased grain imports. Such policies seldom reach into the rural areas where needs are greatest, and in cities they tend to make food artificially cheap for everyone, not only the poor. This pleases powerful urban groups: labor unions, civil servants, university students, and the police.

Micronutrient deficits have also been addressed by policy interventions in the developing world through the fortification of flour with iron, folic acid, or vitamin B, usually at centralized industrial milling facilities. This is a relatively inexpensive process (it adds only a tiny fraction of a penny to the cost of a loaf of bread) and effective for those who get the fortified flour, but it often excludes the rural economy where milling is small scale and localized.

Supporting broadly based income growth is the best way to address chronic undernutrition in poor countries. In the poorest agricultural societies, in Asia and Africa, this requires in the first instance an increase in the productivity of land and labor in the farming sector. As long as agricultural labor earns only about $1 a day, the vast majority of rural citizens who work as farmers will remain poor and hence vulnerable to chronic undernutrition. Rural poverty and hunger worsened in sub-Saharan Africa in the 1980s and 1990s largely because average value added per farmworker per year was low and during some periods actually falling (e.g., from $418 in 1980 to just $379 by 1997). In East Asia, where hunger was in decline, average value added per farmworker was increasing sharply during this same period (up by 50 percent in Thailand and up by 100 percent in China). Increasing the productivity of farm labor typically requires the introduction of new technologies such as improved seeds, fertilizers, and machinery. It also requires government investment in basic rural public goods such as roads and electricity. It is because so few of these things have been provided that farm productivity in Africa remains low, and people remain poor and hungry.

5

THE POLITICS OF FAMINE

How does famine differ from chronic undernutrition?

A famine takes place when large numbers of people die quickly because they have not had enough food to eat. Some die from actual starvation—acute wasting—and others die from diseases that attack them in their wasted state. Low food intake continuously afflicts hundreds of millions of poor people in the developing world, but actual famines are now rare. Famine events are specific to a time and place, so they are easy to label and measure: the Irish famine of 1845–49, the Bengal famine of 1943, the Leningrad famine of 1941–44, the Chinese Great Leap Forward famine of 1959–61.

When have famines taken place?

Famine is as old as recorded history. The book of Revelation presents famine as one of the four horsemen of the Apocalypse. Europe suffered a great famine from 1315–17 that killed millions. In France during the Hundred Years War, a combination of warfare, crop failures, and epidemics reduced the population by two-thirds. In Ireland between 1845–49, famine triggered by a recurring potato blight killed 1 million people outright and drove another million from the country as refugees. In China from 1333 to 1337, a famine killed 6 million people. During the first half of the 19th century, famines killed a total of 45 million people in China. In India, there were 14 famines between the 11th and 17th centuries. India's great famine of 1876–78 killed 6 to 10 million people.

By the 20th century, famine had largely disappeared from western Europe, but its effects continued to be felt in Asia, Africa, and also in eastern Europe. In the Soviet Union under Lenin and Stalin, Ukraine experienced a famine in 1921–22 and then more severely in 1932–33. During World War II, the city of Leningrad suffered a famine that killed roughly 1 million people. In Asia, a famine visited Bengal in 1943 and killed 1.5 to 3 million people. Famine devastated China in 1958–61, during Mao Zedong's disastrous Great Leap Forward, killing as many as 30 million people, the single largest famine of the century and probably of all time. Famine returned to Asia in North Korea in 1996–99, with estimated deaths ranging from 200,000 up to 3.5 million. In Africa, famine struck in the Sahel and in Ethiopia in the early 1970s and then again in Ethiopia and Sudan in the 1980s.

What causes famines?

Famines have diverse causes. In some instances, a natural event is the trigger, such as the drought in the African Sahel in the early 1970s that devastated both grain production and the forage needed for animals. In other cases (Ireland in 1845), a crop disease—in this case, a potato blight—can cut food production. In still other cases, such as Bangladesh in 1974, it can be rain-induced flooding, which disrupts agricultural production and drives food prices in the market beyond the reach of the poor. In Ethiopia, Sudan, and Mozambique in the 1980s, adverse impacts from drought were compounded by violent internal conflict. In the Russian city of Leningrad in 1941, famine broke out when a surrounding German army laid siege.

Ideology can cause famine. In Ukraine in 1932–33, Stalin took land and food away from private farmers because he viewed them as "capitalist" enemies of the working class. There was no drought, no blight, no flood, and no war—just a coercive government takeover intended to "socialize" the farming sector. Peasants who resisted were imprisoned or shot. As production fell, forcible state procurements of grain continued, and in one of the richest grain-growing regions of the world, at least 6 million people starved. More than ideological blindness may have been at work. Historian Robert Conquest, author of *Harvest of Sorrow*, has depicted the situation in Ukraine as a "terror famine," an intentional campaign to starve Ukrainians suspected of political disloyalty to Moscow.

The famine in China in 1959–61 was also driven by ideology—in this case, Mao Zedong's 1958 decision to organize food production (and everything else) according to a system of people's communes. Ownership of farmland and control over the food produced were both taken away, moves that eliminated the incentive to be productive. To achieve a so-called Great Leap Forward, peasant farmers also had their labor interrupted by a new requirement that they begin producing steel out of scrap metal in "backyard furnaces." Grain production collapsed in 1959, but requirements by local Communist Party cadres to deliver grain to the state to feed the urban workforce nonetheless increased. This left the peasants with nothing for themselves, and 15 to 30 million starved. Controversy continues to swirl over how much Mao knew of the suffering his policies caused. Jung Chang and Jon Halliday, authors of *Mao: The Unknown Story*, allege that Mao had not intended it but was willing to accept it as a price to be paid for the progress of his revolution. In 1962, Mao was finally forced to abandon the Great Leap Forward policies that were causing the famine.

Despite the multiple causes, some famine scholars have tried to provide generalized explanations. The most prominent modern famine scholar is Amartya Sen, a Bengali economist and philosopher who won a Nobel Prize in 1998 for his contribution to welfare economics. Sen, who witnessed the famine in Bengal in 1943 as a young boy, wrote an important book in 1981 (*Poverty and Famines: An Essay on Entitlement and Deprivation*) challenging the conventional belief that famines are caused by "food availability declines." Sen had found that during the 1943 Bengal famine, locally available food supplies did not decline; the deprivation resulted instead from a surge in wartime spending by Great Britain (Britain had colonized Bengal and was fighting Japan), triggering a pattern of panic buying and hoarding that drove the price of food out of the reach of the poor. As many as 3 million died, even without a food availability decline.

Sen explains a 1974 Bangladesh famine in much the same way. Floods disrupted agricultural labor, which in turn cut the income of landless farmworkers. This also created an expectation of rice shortages, causing hoarding and panic buying and driving prices out of reach of the poor. Vulnerable groups that depended on a particular relationship between the market value of their own labor and the price of rice found that their *exchange entitlement* (Sen's terminology) to food had been taken away. Those with a more direct entitlement to food—for example, those who owned the land that produced food—did not starve.

Sen's warnings of the famine dangers linked to unregulated markets remain popular among academic critics of markets, yet Sen's own later work shifted the emphasis to a warning against undemocratic political systems. Sen observed that undemocratic China had suffered the Great Leap famine even though its markets were heavily regulated, whereas democratic India avoided famine in 1965 and 1966 despite 2 consecutive years of failing monsoon rains. The elected political leaders of India knew their own survival in office required a prompt response to the crisis, so they turned to the outside world for millions of tons of emergency food aid and expanded public food distribution systems. Starvation deaths were avoided. This was a powerful insight. The history of the 20th century suggests that states with either free markets or free elections will be far less famine prone than those with neither. In the most extreme famine cases of Ukraine under Stalin, China under Mao, Ethiopia in the 1980s, Mozambique in the 1980s, and North Korea in the 1990s (all under one-party Communist rule), there were neither free markets nor free elections. In the famine cases of Bengal in 1943 (under British colonial rule, a bit like Ireland in 1845) and Sudan in the 1980s (essentially a military regime), there were free markets but no free elections.

Nondemocratic leaders with personality cults often impose poorly informed schemes on the food and farming sector. One of Stalin's most notorious legacies was his insistence that the study of plant genetics should conform to theories promoted by Trofim Lysenko, a Ukrainian agronomist who believed the inheritance of plant traits could be shaped by environmental influences, a view Stalin favored because it was more "revolutionary." Mao Zedong's regime promoted a system of "close planting and deep-plowing" for rice that damaged production. In 1970, Fidel Castro convulsed the Cuban economy by setting an impossibly high sugar-production goal of 10 million tons. In 1973–76, President Julius Nyerere of Tanzania disrupted food production in his country by resettling smallholder farmers, often against their will, into more centralized Ujamaa villages. North Korean leader Kim Jong Il personally promulgated instructions on correct methods of potato farming in the midst of his country's famine in 1998.

How do famines end?

Famines can end for nearly as many different reasons as they begin. In the case of Ireland, famine deaths declined in part because many fled the country (including a large emigration to the United States) and also because so many potential victims had already died. In addition, Britain finally responded by sending food and funds to help Ireland, so by 1849–50, public workhouses were able to care for those left destitute by the continuing crop failures.

In the case of Ukraine, by 1933, roughly 25 percent of the population had already perished, including nearly all of the propertied farmers who had resisted the move toward socialized agriculture. Once private agriculture had been destroyed and his political objectives achieved, Stalin reduced mandatory state procurements from the region and allowed food distribution to resume, so the famine subsided. In the case of the Bengal famine of 1943, the crisis ended when the government in London finally accepted the need to import 1 million tons of grain to Bengal, which discouraged hoarding and brought food prices back down to a level the poor could afford. In the case of Mao's famine in China, an abandonment of the Great Leap policies, a decision to permit grain imports, and a reduction in mandatory state procurements were all key to ending the starvation.

In the case of the African Sahel, surviving pastoralist populations first relocated southward to less drought-prone regions, and then fortunately, the cyclical rains improved. In the case of Ethiopia, Sudan, and Mozambique in the 1980s, famines that were largely triggered by drought and civil conflict ended when the rains returned or the civil conflicts diminished. In the case of North Korea, as noted earlier, famine conditions subsided when international food aid began to arrive and when the regime temporarily relaxed its command economy and allowed some foods to be sold privately.

What has been the most successful international response to famine?

The international response to famine that has met with the most long-term success has been to deliver food and medical aid but not too soon or for too long. If international food aid is distributed at feeding stations in rural market towns too soon after a drought, some people who are not yet starving will be tempted to leave their farms and relocate to these feeding stations in search of free food, water, and medicine. This is a dangerous development because these farmers will then be away from their fields when the rains return the next season, and they will not be in a position to plant a new crop. They will become permanently dependent on food aid. Dislocation should be avoided as long as food-stressed populations are still "coping."

Fortunately, a wide range of coping strategies are usually available in impoverished countries when food shortages loom, including eating fewer meals every day, switching to less desirable "famine foods" (including wild foods that can be foraged or hunted in the bush), and selling off some animals or some nonessential household assets, such as jewelry, to raise the money needed to purchase food. Only when people run out of such options and begin taking more drastic steps, such as selling off essential farm implements, should they be encouraged to relocate near feeding camps, and they should then be kept in this dependent condition only as long as necessary (so the food aid deliveries should not continue on an open-ended basis). Once the rains return or once the violent conflict ends, internally displaced people should return to their farming communities. This is best done by replacing the food aid with a one-time distribution of farm implements, animals, and cash, the things people will need to return to a productive livelihood.

Can famines be prevented?

Famines are now prevented on a regular basis. In Africa, famines linked to drought that once seemed inevitable have recently been avoided thanks to greatly improved systems that give early warning when a drought-induced food shortage is about to emerge. In addition, there are far more effective international institutions for the delivery of emergency food aid. These important international capabilities did not exist in 1972–74, when an estimated 300,000 Africans died during a drought emergency in the Sahel. Nor were they fully in place in the mid-1980s, when a much wider drought in eastern as well as western Africa forced more than 10 million farmers to abandon their land and brought death to as many as 1 million. Outsiders watched helplessly on television as the tragedy unfolded.

Having learned from these traumatizing events in the 1970s and 1980s, the international community resolved to put in place for Africa a famine early warning system (FEWS) based on regular assessments of local rainfall patterns and market prices to ensure a more effective response to future drought emergencies. This system, operated by the UN Food and Agriculture Organization (FAO) and the U.S. Agency for International Development (USAID), proved successful in giving advance warning of food aid needs when drought struck southern Africa in 1991–92. In Malawi, Namibia, Swaziland, and Zimbabwe, cereal production fell 60–70 percent, and throughout the region, 17–20 million people were placed at starvation risk. Yet thanks to an effective food aid response from the UN World Food Programme (WFP) working in cooperation with local governments and humanitarian relief nongovernmental organizations (NGOs), the only famine deaths reported were in Mozambique, where aid was impossible to deliver because of an ongoing civil war. This new international capacity to prevent famine in Africa was then successfully tested a second time in southern Africa in 2001–2, when drought returned and 15 million people were put at starvation risk. Once again, the international food aid response was timely, and essentially, no famine deaths occurred.

This new international famine-prevention capacity can falter badly, however, in countries torn by internal conflict, for example, Sudan, where a war has been waged since 2003 by government-sponsored Afro-Arab Janjaweed militia fighters against separatist farming communities in the Darfur region. This war killed at least 200,000 people through 2008 and drove 2.5 million more from their homes into refugee camps or across the border into Chad. Some 3 million people were kept alive by food aid delivered through the WFP and a network of international humanitarian NGOs, but in 2008, the WFP had to cut its food aid deliveries to Darfur by 50 percent due to relentless attacks on food convoys. By September 2008, the WFP had reported 69 hijacked trucks, with 43 of the drivers missing. In 2009, the crisis worsened when the government in Khartoum expelled private aid groups from the country.

Authoritarian states often deny relief workers adequate freedom to operate. The North Korean regime was willing to accept food aid off and on during its famine in the late 1990s, but for years it refused international aid workers access to its internal distribution systems or to the regions in the northern part of the country where famine conditions were most acute. The WFP asked for on-the-ground access to all storage and distribution sites, a condition the North Koreans were not willing to fulfill, resulting in a dispute over access that led the North Koreans to expel WFP representatives from the country in 2005. In 2008, with more than one-third of its population still in need of food aid, North Korea finally granted improved access to the WFP.

Governments such as those in North Korea and Sudan are fortunately the exception today. Chronic undernutrition is still a massive problem in regions such as sub-Saharan Africa and South Asia, but actual famine has become rare.

6

THE GREEN REVOLUTION CONTROVERSY

What was the original green revolution?

The original green revolution was an introduction of newly developed wheat and rice seeds into Latin America and into the irrigated farming lands of South and Southeast Asia in the 1960s and 1970s. These new seed varieties were created by plant breeders working in Mexico and the Philippines with support from the Rockefeller Foundation. The seeds were capable of producing much higher yields when grown with adequate water and fertilizer. The plant breeders, by crossing different varieties, managed to incorporate dwarfing genes into the plants, producing short stiff-strawed varieties that devoted more energy to producing grain and less to straw or leaf material. The short stiff straws also helped hold the heavier weight of grain.

Wheat farmers in India began planting these new varieties in 1964, and by 1970, production had nearly doubled. The new rice seeds gave an equally spectacular performance. In India, rice production doubled between 1971 and 1976 in the states of Punjab and Haryana. In Asia overall, rice output had increased at only a 2.1 percent annual rate during the two decades before the new varieties were introduced in 1965, but then it grew at a 2.9 percent annual rate for the next two decades. This significant increase in Asia's capacity to produce basic grains came at a critical time, when rates of population growth were at a peak. Supporters of these new seeds credit them with saving Asia from what would have been a tragic food crisis. In 1970, the American scientist who did the most to develop and promote the new wheat varieties, Norman Borlaug, was awarded a Nobel Peace Prize.

The green revolution did not end with wheat and rice. Significantly improved varieties of sorghum, millet, and barley, and improved varieties of root crops such as cassava, were eventually developed in the 1980s. Overall, more than 8,000 new seed varieties were introduced for at least 11 different crops. Robert Evenson, an economist at Yale University, concluded in 2003 that if these modern varieties had not been introduced after 1965, annual crop production in the developing world would have been 16–19 percent lower in the year 2000.

Why is the green revolution controversial?

Despite offering dramatic production gains, the new seeds of the green revolution were surrounded by political controversy from the start. Some critics feared they would lead to greater income inequality if only larger farmers were able to adopt them. Others worried they would make farmers too dependent on the purchase of expensive inputs such as fertilizer. Still others feared environmental damage from excessive fertilizer applications, excessive pumping of groundwater for irrigation, or excessive spraying of pesticides. The new seeds were also criticized on grounds that they would reduce biodiversity when uniform monocultures of green revolution varieties replaced diverse polycultures of traditional crop varieties.

Critics even tried to argue that green revolution seeds were a cause of violent conflicts in India between Hindus and Muslims in the Punjab and of revolutionary struggles that swept through Central America in the 1980s.

At the foundation of much of this criticism is a widespread social suspicion, mostly among nonfarmers, of any new technology that employs science to alter or dominate the biology of traditional farming. It is not an accident that green revolution critics also tend to criticize most other 20th-century agricultural innovations, including synthetic nitrogen fertilizers, chemical pesticides, and of course, genetically engineered seeds. They favor instead traditional seed varieties developed and selected by farmers themselves based on "indigenous knowledge" rather than laboratory science. Most of these critics are not farmers themselves, but they express sympathy for the smaller and more diversified farmers of the past who purchased fewer inputs and sold their output locally.

This fundamental question of what an ideal farming system should look like explains a great deal of the modern politics of food and agriculture. Advocates for the green revolution approach look for ways to bring a farm technology upgrade to sub-Saharan Africa, the one region not reached by the original green revolution, but they encounter critics arguing against this objective. When the Rockefeller Foundation and the Bill and Melinda Gates Foundation formed a partnership in 2006 called the Alliance for a Green Revolution in Africa (AGRA), the initiative brought immediate criticism from activist groups. Peter Rosset, speaking for a nongovernmental organization (NGO) in the United States named Food First, warned that the most likely result of the new initiative would be "higher profits for the seed and fertilizer industries, negligible impacts on total food production and a worsening exclusion and marginalization in the countryside."

These dramatically divergent opinions about the green revolution can also be explained by the divergent performance of the new seeds in Asia versus Latin America. People who work in Asia generally like the green revolution, but those who work in Latin America often do not. This is because the benefits of the new seed varieties in Asia were widely shared by the poor, whereas in Latin America, the poor gained very little. Advocates for the green revolution approach usually draw their arguments from the experience of Asia, while critics refer more often to what went wrong in Latin America.

Did the original green revolution lead to greater rural inequality?

It did in Latin America but not in Asia. Outcomes differ in these two regions largely due to differing patterns of inequality in the countryside. In much of Latin America, the ownership of productive land and access to credit for the purchase of essential green revolution inputs such as fertilizer tend to be restricted to a privileged rural elite. If a highly productive new technology becomes available within such an inequitable system, only the narrow elite will make effective use of the technology, and as a result, inequality will worsen. In most of Asia, by contrast, access to good agricultural land and credit was not as narrowly controlled, which allowed the uptake of the new seeds to be more widely shared and brought more equitable gains in the end.

The history of farming in Latin America is one of social injustice. The indigenous population went into a tragic decline soon after the voyages of Columbus, dropping an estimated 75 percent by 1650 due to a combination of brutal treatment

by the Spanish and Portuguese conquerors plus deadly exposure to unfamiliar European diseases. The Europeans replaced
indigenous societies with vast semifeudal *hacienda* estates, on
which peasants farmed small plots for subsistence purposes
without any secure rights to land or anything else. To the
present day, ownership of the best land in Latin America
remains in the hands of a small commercial farming elite, and
large numbers of poor peasants own very little land or no land
at all. For every 100 smallholder farmers who do own some
land in the Latin American countryside, 82 others do not.

The introduction of green revolution technologies worsened these rural inequities. The commercial farming elite
adopted the new seeds quickly, partly because they received
subsidies to help purchase fertilizers, pesticides, and the new
seeds. Additionally, they received subsidized credits from the
government, research and extension assistance, new irrigation canals for their land, and exemptions from import duties
on farm tractors. Agricultural land was made more valuable
by the new seeds, but this backfired on the poor who had
previously been allowed to subsist on land they did not own.
They were now pushed off by the landlords to make way for
expanded commercial production. Some of the evicted peasants gained limited compensation in the form of seasonal
employment as hired cotton pickers, but otherwise they were
forced to move their farming efforts onto lands with irregular
terrain, no access to irrigation, and less fertile soil. Or they
became slum dwellers on the fringes of the urban economy.

Asia had a dramatically different experience with the green
revolution seeds because farming in this region is more often
dominated by small farmers with irrigation, and there are
fewer large estates. Because the new seeds were a biological
technology, it was not necessary to have a large farm to make

use of them (the opposite is true for mechanical technologies such as tractors). Tenant farmers who rented land could also use the seeds as long as they had irrigation and could get access to credit. In fact, in one study of 36 rice-growing villages in India between 1966 and 1972, it was found that small farms (less than 1 hectare in size) adopted the new seeds more quickly than larger farms (over 3 hectares in size). The higher yielding green revolution varieties also brought a substantial increase in annual farm labor use per unit of cropped land, pushing up rural wages to the benefit of the landless poor.

Critics try to ignore these gains. In 1992, long after the results of green revolution technology were shown in Asia, celebrity activist Vandana Shiva published a polemic titled *The Violence of the Green Revolution* depicting the new seeds as a plot by multinational companies (the seeds had actually been introduced by philanthropic foundations and governments) to lure farmers away from growing traditional crops, destroying their culture and making them poor and dependent. Poverty has declined significantly in rural Asia since the green revolution, and farmers have shown no interest in abandoning the seeds, yet many activist groups remain hostile. In 2004, a coalition of 670 separate NGOs sent an open letter to the director general of the UN Food and Agriculture Organization (FAO) that referred to the green revolution as a "tragedy."

Was the green revolution bad for the environment?

Environmental outcomes also differed in Latin America versus Asia. In Latin America, two different kinds of environmental damage from green revolution farming tended to emerge side by side. On the best lands controlled by politically favored elites, government subsidies induced farmers to employ too much irrigation, too much nitrogen fertilizer, and too many chemical pesticides, which led to occupational hazards on the farm and the pollution of surface waters downstream. In Mexico between 1961 and 1989, fertilizer subsidies led to an 800 percent increase in nitrogen fertilizer use per hectare, and in the decade of the 1970s, pesticide use—again, subsidized—increased at an average annual rate of more than 8 percent. In the Culiacan Valley, commercial tomato growers began spraying pesticides on their crops as often as 25 to 50 times each growing season.

A different kind of environmental damage was done in Latin America by poor farmers who were denied subsidies and were confined to sloping or nonirrigated lands. These farmers used too little fertilizer rather than too much, exhausting the soils and forcing them to move onto even more fragile lands or into the forest margins. In Honduras, where population doubled between 1970 and 1990 and where the poorest two-thirds of all farmers had to share just 10 percent of the nation's total farming area, destitute peasants eroded or exhausted their poor soils and cut much of the remaining forest. In Mexico, where half of all farmers were trying to subsist on only 10 percent of the nation's farmland, population growth among the rural poor led to a spread of traditional low-yield farming techniques that devastated the environment. In the Mixteca region, 70 percent of the potentially arable land lost its ability to grow crops due to soil erosion, and large parts of rural Mexico came to resemble a lifeless moonscape.

In some parts of Asia, the green revolution also brought excessive water and pesticide use, often due to unwise government subsidies just as in Latin America. In Punjab in northwest India in the 1980s, the government paid 86 percent of the electric bill for pumping irrigation water as a reward to politically powerful commercial farm interests—resulting in excess water use and a precipitous drop in groundwater tables. In the early 1980s, the government of Indonesia subsidized fertilizer purchases by 68 percent, causing fertilizer use to increase by more than two-thirds, which increased nitrates in drinking water and brought excessive nutrients to streams and ponds, resulting in damaging algae growth. Indonesia also offered an 85 percent subsidy to farmers who purchased pesticides, and excessive spraying on rice fields killed the good insects and the spiders that had earlier helped keep bad insects (brown planthoppers) under control, while the bad insects evolved to resist the chemical sprays. The government was finally forced in 1986 to ban the spraying of 57 different insecticides on rice, a move that allowed the natural enemies of the hoppers to recover and brought the damage under control.

As serious as these problems were in Asia, the only thing more damaging to the rural environment might have been to introduce no high-yield seeds at all. If India had relied on its traditional low-yield farming techniques to achieve the production increase it needed during these decades of rapid population growth, it would have had no choice but to cut more trees, destroy more wildlife habitat, and plow up more fragile sloping and dryland soils. In 1964, India produced 12 million tons of wheat on 14 million hectares of land. Thirty years later, thanks to the green revolution, India produced 57 million tons of wheat on 24 million hectares of land. To produce this much wheat using the old seeds would have required roughly 60 million hectares, more than doubling the area under the plow. M. S. Swaminathan, one of the scientists who led the green revolution in India, concluded, "Thanks to plant breeding, a tremendous onslaught on fragile lands and forest margins has been avoided."

Why did the original green revolution not reach Africa?

Green revolution farming has not yet reached deeply into sub-Saharan Africa. Between 1970 and 1998, while the share of cropped area planted to modern green revolution varieties increased to 82 percent in the developing regions of Asia and up to 52 percent in Latin America, only 27 percent of area was planted to such varieties in sub-Saharan Africa. As a consequence, average cereal yields in Africa remained at only 1.1 tons per hectare versus 2.8 tons per hectare in Latin America and 3.7 tons per hectare in Asia. Also as a consequence, growth in per capita food production in sub-Saharan Africa was actually negative between 1980 and 2000, and one-third of all Africans remain undernourished.

Efforts were made to introduce green revolution seed varieties into Africa in the 1960s and 1970s, but there was little adoption because the international assistance agencies introducing the varieties had tried to "shortcut" the time-consuming process of identifying and using locally adapted plants as the starting point for breeding improvements. Varieties not suited to African conditions were brought in from Latin America and Asia, and African farmers did not like them. This problem was belatedly addressed through breeding programs that were more location specific beginning in the 1980s, but by that time, international assistance for such programs had begun to decline because the so-called world food crisis of the 1970s was deemed by rich donor governments to be over.

African farmers also failed to take up the new seed varieties because they had a more complex mix of agroecologies, and a smaller share of their land was suited to conventional irrigation. Access to farmland is generally more equitable than in either Latin America or Asia, but only 4 percent of agricultural land in Africa is irrigated. This forces farmers to rely on uncertain rainfall and weakens their incentive to invest in improved green revolution seeds, which only do well with adequate moisture. In addition, the dominant food crops in the region included root crops like sweet potato and cassava, or tropical white maize, rather than the leading green revolution cereal crops such as wheat, rice, and yellow maize. Critical as well, most farmers in Africa are women, lacking the political voice needed to demand government investments in rural education, road infrastructure, and electrical power of the kind that were essential to the earlier uptake of the technology in Asia.

What approaches do green revolution critics favor?

Critics of the green revolution argue that rural poverty can be reduced and farm productivity can be increased without bringing in new seeds that rely on heavier fertilizer use. They prefer farming models based on *agroecology*, an approach that favors small diversified farms over large specialized farms, polycultures over monocultures, biological controls for pests rather than chemical controls, crop rotations and manuring to replace soil nutrients rather than synthetic nitrogen fertilizers, mulching and water-harvesting systems over large-scale irrigation, and community-based or indigenous knowledge over laboratory science. Agroecology advocates believe efforts to engineer natural biological systems will always produce unintended consequences, many of them bad. Instead of trying to dominate nature, farmers should be learning from and even imitating nature.

In Latin America, where the green revolution is easy to attack, the most prominent advocate of agroecology is Miguel Altieri, an ecosystem biologist originally from Chile, who promotes the enhancement of traditional or indigenous knowledge systems as an alternative to exotic, reductionist approaches. The greatest strength of this work is its effort to balance a search for short-term productivity with an insistence on long-term stability, social equity, and sustainability. Green revolution advocates would counter that their approach can also be stable, equitable, and sustainable, assuming equal access to land and credit plus continuing research investments to develop new seed varieties so as to stay ahead of evolving pest and disease pressures. Agroecologists doubt the ability of science to stay ahead of such pressures forever.

Advocates for agroecology have gained prominent endorsements for their approach. For example, an International Assessment of Agricultural Knowledge, Science and Technology for Development (IAASTD) completed in 2008 warned that relying on science and technology to increase agricultural productivity would bring too many "unintended social and environmental consequences." This assessment, conducted under the auspices of the World Bank and the United Nations, asserted that the model of innovation that drove the original green revolution "requires revision." It called for more emphasis on agroecological approaches, organic approaches, and the incorporation of "traditional and local knowledge." This assessment was rejected by green revolution advocates, who complained it had been too heavily shaped by nonscientists, including environmental advocates from NGOs such as Greenpeace International, Friends of the Earth International, and the Pesticide Action Network.

Pure agroecological approaches do tend to be far less productive than green revolution approaches because they reject the use of off-farm inputs like nitrogen fertilizer, making soil-nutrient replacement more costly, and they make much larger demands on farm labor. Most smallholder farmers in Africa today practice something that seems suspiciously close to pure agroecology: They use traditional seeds, plant their crops in polycultures, harvest rainfall, purchase almost no inputs such as nitrogen fertilizers or pesticides from off the farm, and work from dawn to dusk. The result is that their cereal crop yields are only 10–20 percent as high as in North America, they earn only $1 a day on average, and one-third are undernourished. The best approach is usually to combine agroecological insights with green revolution seeds and off-farm inputs. For example, integrated pest management (IPM) combines important agroecological approaches (biological controls and intensive monitoring of pest pressures) with green revolution seeds plus the limited use of chemical pesticides as a last resort. So-called conventional farms in Europe and North America have long used agroecological techniques such as crop rotations, cover crops, and manuring. As for equity and sustainability issues, these are sometimes best addressed through interventions that go beyond the realm of technology, such as programs that give the poor improved access to land and credit.

How have green revolution critics shaped international policy?

Political controversies over green revolution farming continue to rage in a number of important settings among foreign aid donors and within intergovernmental organizations. In such settings, nongovernmental organizations that reject the green revolution fight hard to promote agroecological and organic approaches to farming and to block green revolution approaches that rely on purchased inputs and modern agricultural science. In the 1980s, this kind of political advocacy against the green revolution began to have an impact on the foreign assistance policies of donor countries. Assistance to promote irrigation, new seed distribution, and access to chemical fertilizers was cut back.

Between 1980 and 2003, the real dollar value of all bilateral assistance to help modernize agriculture in the developing world declined by 64 percent, from $5.3 billion (in constant 1999 U.S. dollars) to only $1.9 billion. United States assistance to agricultural research in Africa specifically declined by 77 percent. This withdrawal of donor support had little effect in Latin America and Asia, where agricultural modernization was already successfully under way, but it left the aid-dependent governments in Africa without enough external support to begin a confident move down a green revolution path.

Criticism of the green revolution is pervasive in the environmental community. In 1992, Senator Al Gore, soon to become vice president, published a best-selling book titled *Earth in the Balance* that depicted the green revolution as a dangerous Faustian bargain, one that used environmentally unsustainable, science-based techniques to secure only temporary gains in output. In fact, the yield gains were not temporary in Asia (yields continue to increase), and in Africa the lack of a green revolution has yielded essentially no gains at all. Yet Gore's view is now surprisingly dominant among those who are not farming specialists. Later in the 1990s, one of the architects of the original green revolution in Asia, Gordon Conway, tried to rescue science-based farming from its critics by calling for research investments in a "doubly green revolution" that would increase yields while at the same time protect the environment and ensure benefits for the poor, but support for international agricultural research continued to fall.

The green revolution approach remains under its political cloud despite the momentarily high food prices of 2008, which were widely described as the harbinger of a new world food crisis. Green revolution advocates responded with a call for more investment in agricultural science to address the looming food deficits, but critics countered with an argument of their own that the crisis revealed the bankruptcy of the green revolution model. The 2008 IAASTD report that endorsed greater emphasis on agroecological approaches was unveiled at the peak of this crisis.

The green revolution is highly controversial in elite circles, especially among environmentalists in rich countries, yet it remains firmly established as the approach of choice among most farmers and agricultural policy leaders, including those in the developing world. In China and India today, green revolution seed varieties grown in monocultures with nitrogen fertilizer are pervasive in food production and are promoted strongly by the state. In fact, China and India are now both moving beyond the original green revolution seed varieties to embrace the latest science-based approach to agriculture: improvement of seeds through genetic engineering (discussed in chapter 13).

7

FOOD AID AND FOOD POWER

What is food aid?

Food aid is the international shipment of food not through commercial channels but through "concessional" channels, as a gift. The food can be given from a donor government to a recipient government, from a donor government to a nongovernmental organization (NGO) working inside the recipient country, or by a multilateral organization such as the World Food Programme (WFP) of the United Nations. The food can be sourced from government-owned surplus supplies, purchased in the home market of the donor country, purchased from a local market in the recipient country, or purchased in a third-country market close to the recipient country. The purpose of the food aid can be to address a temporary famine emergency, to cushion food price inflation (as in the case of the 2008 world food crisis), to feed a dependent refugee population, or to support local work or education activities (through "food for work" programs or school lunch programs). It can generate cash income through local sales into the market (monetization), dispose of a surplus, or in some cases, reward recipient governments for taking foreign policy actions pleasing to the donor government. Because there are so many ways to give food aid and so many different reasons for giving it, general-izations usually fail.

However, one generalization does work. As a share of all cross-border food shipments, the food aid share is no longer of great significance. In the early 1970s, international food aid still made up about 10 percent of all cross-border food flows, but food aid declined in relative importance as commercial trade expanded, and now it makes up only about 3 percent of total cross-border food flows. Food aid does, however, remain a significant share of total food imports for some individual recipient countries.

Which countries get food aid?

In the early 1950s, the most important recipients of interna-tional food aid were in Europe and East Asia. Most of the food came from the United States to support reconstruction in these regions (e.g., under the Marshall Plan) following the damage of World War II. By the 1960s, the focus of most food aid had shifted to India and South Asia. In the 1970s and 1980s, a great deal of American food aid went to Vietnam and to the Middle East in service of foreign policy objectives. By the 1990s, sub-Saharan Africa had become the target destina-tion for most food aid. According to one calculation done in the mid-1990s, concessional international food aid provided more than 40 percent of total cereal imports for more than 40 recipient countries, most of them in Africa.

Food aid today moves less through bilateral government-to-government channels and more through the UN World Food Programme. Following an important UN World Food Conference in 1974, during the world food crisis of that decade, the WFP began to take over an increased share of world food aid flows, and by 2000, roughly 38 percent of all global food aid was delivered by the WFP. Today, the WFP's share is up to 55 percent. National governments in rich countries still fund nearly all food aid, but two-thirds of this aid is now distributed either by the WFP or by NGOs rather than government to government. The enlarged role of the WFP has helped diminish the role of crude foreign policy calculations in determining who gets aid and who does not. Unfortunately, this makes it easier for recipient countries to grow comfortable depending on food aid. In the 1960s, when most food aid came straight from the U.S. government with diplomatic and foreign policy strings attached, recipient countries such as India became unhappy with the relationship and, partly to escape a dependence on food aid, made larger investments in their own agricultural production. Governments in Africa today that depend on food aid have shown less urgency in reducing their dependence because the food is coming to them from the United Nations without any political conditioning.

Do rich countries give food aid to dispose of their surplus production?

In the United States, when farm subsidy policies began to generate surplus quantities of wheat in the 1950s, international food aid was one way to get that surplus out of government storage bins. Under Public Law 480 enacted in 1954, also known as the Food for Peace program, government-owned surplus commodities were shipped directly to recipient governments in the developing world. To avoid complaints of unfair trade from export competitors, and also to respect sensitivities in recipient countries, "payment" was accepted for the food in nonconvertible local currencies that could only be spent by the U.S. embassy inside the local economy. Because long-term and low-interest credit terms were also allowed, the food was essentially given away free.

The P.L. 480 program played a significant role in helping the U.S. government dispose of its grain surplus when commercial export markets were not growing. By 1960, fully 70 percent of U.S. wheat exports were moving abroad as concessional food aid rather than commercial sales. Later in the 1960s, when the United States began supporting farm income with cash payments rather than by purchases of grain, the amount of surplus food owned by the government declined, but the food aid program by then had become a convenient tool in the conduct of American foreign policy, so it did not disappear. By the 1970s, the government-owned grain surplus was gone, but Congress authorized continuing the program based on purchases of food in the marketplace as long as it was purchased in the United States and shipped in U.S. vessels.

Why are America's food aid policies so difficult to change?

America's method of giving food aid has changed little since the 1970s. To the present day, most of the food is purchased in the United States and most of it is shipped in U.S. vessels. It would be far less costly to purchase the food closer to the site of the emergency, and every other donor country, including the European countries, Japan, and now even Canada, has moved toward local purchase as the best practice for food aid, but rules set by Congress prevent the United States from doing the same.

Changing these rules will not be easy. In 2006 and 2007, President George W. Bush attempted to allocate a small percentage of the food aid budget for procurements abroad, but Congress said no. This is not a partisan issue. Former President Bill Clinton said it was to Bush's "everlasting credit" that he had at least challenged Congress on the issue. A second provision that will be hard to change is a legal requirement that 75 percent of all gross tonnage of food aid be transported on U.S.-flag vessels, which are 70 to 80 percent more costly per ton than foreign-flag carriers. The Department of Defense joins the shipping lobby in favoring this provision because it helps keep an American merchant fleet in operation to provide secure ocean transport in the event of a future military conflict, so efforts to repeal "cargo preference" always fall short in Congress. Because international purchase is not allowed and because so much shipment on U.S.-flag vessels is required, roughly 65 percent of America's food aid spending is eaten up by administrative and transport costs.

Another dubious feature of American food aid is a frequent practice of selling the food into local markets rather than targeting deliveries to needy recipients. Over one recent 3-year period, more than $500 million worth of American food aid was "monetized" in this fashion. This practice lowers local food prices for the well-to-do as well as for the poor and hungry, and it undercuts market prices to the disadvantage of local farmers. By discouraging local food production, the monetization practice tends to prolong local dependence on food aid. This practice persists because some of the American NGOs handling the food rely on proceeds from the sales to fund their other local development projects. A number of leading American NGOs, including CARE, Catholic Relief Services, and Save the Children, have recently signed a declaration, along with British, French, and Canadian aid groups, calling this practice into question.

If Congress were to ban monetization, end cargo preference for U.S. vessels, and allow food purchases to be made outside the United States, America's food aid programs would make far better use of each dollar spent. Realistically, however, many fewer dollars would probably be spent. The farm lobby, the shipping lobby, the Department of Defense, and even some food relief NGOs would be less inclined to support a large budget for food aid under these circumstances. America's budget for food aid is larger than that of any other country (the United States provides roughly 60 percent of all international food aid all by itself) in part because its methods of purchasing and delivering the food are so self-serving.

Does food aid create dependence or hurt farmers in recipient countries?

In the early days of food aid in the 1950s and 1960s, when large shipments of surplus grain were first sent to the developing world as food aid, critics warned that a costly and dangerous dependence might result. Local consumers would become hooked on cheap food delivered from abroad, and local farmers would go out of business due to depressed food prices in the marketplace. Some suspected this was precisely the intent. Once the recipients had been lured into a dependence on food aid, the aid would be taken away, and they would be forced to graduate to the status of paying customers.

Agricultural lobby groups in the United States have often hoped food aid would work in this manner as commercial export promotion, but it seldom has. America's largest food aid shipments in the past have gone to Peru, Haiti, India, Indonesia, Vietnam, Jordan, Egypt, and the Philippines, and none of these later became a leading commercial market for agricultural sales. Because more than half of all food aid displaces imports that would have been purchased otherwise, it can destroy more commercial sales in the short run than it ever creates in the long run. The commercial sales displaced include those of competing exporters, making food aid a contentious issue in international trade. Where commercial sales do grow in the long run, it is usually a result of income growth and more food demand, so development assistance is a far better means of commercial export promotion than food aid.

Even as a subsidy to domestic farmers, food aid today has limited benefits. This is because food aid shipments are now so small relative to the total U.S. farm sales. In 2001, the federal government's total spending on food aid was $1.8 billion, barely noticeable alongside that year's $60 billion in regular commercial exports from U.S. farmers or alongside the $900 billion in total commercial sales made in the domestic U.S. market. The economic benefits of food aid in the United States are salient to the shipping interests that handle the transport, and to the NGOs that raise revenue from monetization, but not to many farmers.

There are some examples of food aid altering the behavior of consumers and food producers in recipient countries. Large deliveries of wheat and rice into West Africa in the 1970s accelerated local shifts in consumer demand away from sorghum and millet toward breads made from wheat. Large deliveries of maize as food aid to the Horn of Africa encouraged recipients, many pastoralists, to shift their diet from animal products to grains. In most recipient countries, however, the food aid delivered is not large enough inside the local market to trigger a significant shift in consumer behavior. Even in some of the poorest recipient countries such as Ethiopia, only about one in ten local recipients receives enough food aid (in value terms) to constitute more than one-quarter of individual income. Displaced communities given food aid at refugee camps can develop a dangerous dependence on the handouts, but not entire national populations.

As for local farmers, when unusually large quantities of food aid are delivered in an untargeted manner or at the wrong time—corresponding with a local harvest—damage can be done. Yet many poor local farmers are themselves purchasers of food during much of the year, so food aid deliveries that are well timed can help them by keeping the local price of food down during the off season, when they have nothing to sell anyway. Still, there are instances when poorly timed or poorly targeted food aid did lead to local production disincentives, including the large shipments of food aid that went to Russia in the 1990s when the cold war ended or large shipments to Ethiopia in 1999–2000 that arrived at the wrong time and collapsed local sorghum prices. Such problems are better contained today because more food aid is delivered for humanitarian purposes rather than as crude surplus disposal and more often through multilateral humanitarian agencies or NGOs that incorporate targeting into their programs. These organizations also do a better job today of controlling the timing of delivery thanks to increasingly sophisticated famine early warning systems (FEWS).

Do governments seek coercive power from food aid and food trade?

Governments are sometimes tempted to seek a coercive advantage by manipulating—or threatening to manipulate—the volume and timing of their food exports. When exporters do this, they are seeking to exercise what has been called *food power*. Yet the historical record shows exporting governments seldom threaten this kind of manipulation, and even less often do they carry through with such threats. On the rare occasions when they do seek to exercise food power, coercive advantages are seldom gained, which is one reason the tactic is so rare.

The temptation to exercise coercive food power has presented itself in the past most often to the United States, the world's largest supplier of both commercial food sales and food aid. On one noted occasion in 1965–68, President Lyndon Johnson gave in to this temptation in his dealings with India by conditioning the continued delivery of food aid on reforms the United States wanted to see in Indian agricultural policy and on reduced Indian criticism of Johnson's war policies in Vietnam. India had suffered two sequential harvest failures in 1965 and 1966 and was heavily dependent on food aid deliveries of wheat from the United States. Thus, it did agree to some of the agricultural policy reforms, which proved good for India in the end, but it was deeply resentful of the coercion and refused to end criticism of American policies in Vietnam. The diplomatic outcome has intensified Indian hostility toward the United States, not subservience.

An even more prominent food power failure was the 1980 effort by President Jimmy Carter to punish the Soviet Union for its invasion of Afghanistan with a partial embargo on U.S. commercial grain exports, mostly wheat and corn. Carter's hope was that a cut in imports would oblige the Soviets to reduce the feeding of grain to cattle and pigs, resulting in meat shortages that might then reduce internal support for the Communist regime. The U.S. embargo failed when other grain-exporting countries—particularly Argentina, Australia, and Canada—agreed to sell more to the Soviets to make up for the U.S. sales being blocked. The Soviets, by offering only small price premiums to these other suppliers, were able to import roughly the same total quantity of grain during the U.S. embargo as they had imported before the embargo. The Soviets even gained an opportunity to blame some meat shortages they were experiencing for other reasons on Jimmy Carter.

In the end, this 1980 grain embargo damaged almost nobody in commercial terms, as U.S. grain exporters redirected their sales to customers temporarily abandoned by Argentina, Australia, and Canada. Everyone had changed partners, but everyone was still dancing. American farmers nonetheless deeply resented President Carter's effort to use their commercial sales as a foreign policy tool, so they voted in large numbers in the 1980 presidential election for Republican candidate Ronald Reagan, who had promised to end the embargo if elected. Reagan was elected, and the embargo was terminated in the first few weeks of his new presidency in 1981. Reagan adopted policies toward the Soviet Union that were far harsher than Carter's in every other area, but when it came to manipulations of commercial food exports, he had concluded there was no foreign policy gain to be made, at least none large enough to justify the wrath of American farmers at home.

Thirty years have now passed since Jimmy Carter's 1980 grain embargo, and no subsequent president has ever repeated the practice of imposing a selective embargo on food exports in hopes of punishing a target country or coercing a policy change. Commercial grain sales have occasionally been blocked for foreign policy purposes in dealings with governments such as North Korea or Cuba, but always as part of a larger across-the-board economic embargo rather than a selective manipulation of food exports.

The fact that governments seldom manipulate food exports in search of a coercive advantage teaches an important lesson about international food markets. Unlike international markets for commodities such as petroleum, markets for food tend to provide little coercive leverage to big exporters. This is because food is not a scarce natural resource available only in a few places in a fixed supply; food is a renewable resource that most countries can and do produce for themselves or can begin to produce. More than 100 countries around the world produce wheat, many for export. In contrast to petroleum, which does not lose its value if left in the ground, food loses value after harvest because it is costly to store without spoilage. Also in contrast to petroleum, food can cause human starvation if withheld, placing a unique stigma on the state that withholds the food. In negotiations with North Korea over food aid, the United States paradoxically finds itself at a disadvantage because any withdrawal of food can be depicted by the North as an American effort to use starvation as a tool of foreign policy, an accusation the United States wishes to avoid. Factors such as these often give food importers more coercive leverage in international markets than exporters. The greatest competition in international food markets is usually not between importers but between exporters.

8
THE POLITICS OF OBESITY

Is the world facing an obesity crisis?

North America and Europe now face a serious and growing health crisis linked to excessive calorie consumption. In some developing countries as well, including Mexico and China, increasing numbers are now experiencing similar problems. In more than 18 countries today, over half of the population is either overweight or obese, and in seven countries (the United States, the United Kingdom, Australia, Egypt, Greece, Mexico, and South Africa), more than two-thirds of all adults are overweight or obese. Worldwide since the 1950s, overweight or obese individuals have increased from fewer than 100 million up to 1.6 billion. This means there are now twice as many seriously overfed people on Earth as there are underfed people. The problem is certain to worsen. The UN World Health Organization (WHO) projects that by 2015 there will be a total of 2.3 billion overweight adults, 700 million of whom will be technically obese. Because so much political attention has traditionally focused on problems of some people having too little food, this new and even larger problem of excessive food consumption has been slow to generate an adequate policy response.

How do we measure obesity?

Obesity is simply the roundness of the body, conventionally measured by health professionals using something called a body mass index (BMI) based on body weight in kilograms divided by the square of height in meters. People with a BMI between 25–30 have traditionally been considered overweight, those with a BMI above 30 are considered obese, and those with a BMI above 40 are considered severely obese. Translating to more familiar measures, a 6-foot-tall individual is considered overweight above 183 pounds, obese above 220 pounds, and severely obese above 295 pounds. Adverse health consequences become far more likely as individuals go from overweight to obese. Obese people in the United States now spend 42 percent more on medical costs than people of normal weight. Obesity, on average, reduces life expectancy by 6 to 7 years.

Between 1971 and 2000, the rate of obesity in the United States doubled from 14.5 percent to 30.9 percent, and 5 percent of all adults are now severely obese. Rates of obesity in Canadian boys increased from 11 percent in the 1980s to over 30 percent in the 1990s, and among Brazilian children from 4 percent to 14 percent during the same period. Racial variations are a factor, as Asians tend to develop adverse health consequences at a lower BMI than Europeans. For this reason, the Japanese have defined obesity as any BMI greater than 25, and China has defined obesity as any BMI greater than 28. Childhood obesity is harder to measure. By some estimates, it increased significantly in the United States after the 1960s and then plateaued at this higher level.

What are the consequences of the obesity epidemic?

Increasingly, obese populations require more medical services to treat ailments such as type 2 diabetes, high blood pressure, and high blood cholesterol. Excess body fat helps explain two-thirds of all cases of diabetes in the United States. One projection based on levels of obesity in the United States in the year 2000 (today's level is higher) estimated that one-third of men and two-fifths of women in the United States would have diabetes before they die. For those who have diabetes, risks of developing heart disease more than double. Obesity and with it diabetes are the only major health problems in the United States that are actually getting worse.

Obesity in childhood is linked to a subsequent risk of coronary heart disease. One projection shows that by 2035 in the United States, largely due to obesity, the prevalence of coronary heart disease will increase significantly, and by 2050, life expectancy may be shortened by 2 to 5 years. Dr. Barry Popkin, director of an interdisciplinary obesity center at the University of North Carolina, explains that sleep problems are also strongly linked to obesity and that obesity is now the single most preventable cause of cancer. In 2006, the head of the EU Directorate for Health and Consumer Affairs announced that obesity had become a bigger killer in Europe than smoking tobacco.

Compounding medical costs make obesity a public health issue, not just a matter for private or family concern. In the United States, the medical costs of treating obesity-related diseases doubled between 1998 and 2008 to reach $147 billion, which is about 9 percent of all medical costs. Obesity also stigmatizes individuals, cutting their employment and income options and often leading them into social isolation and depression. More frequent hospitalizations and more costly medical insurance drive up costs for all and create political demands for a public policy response. In 2009, Thomas Frieden, director of the Centers for Disease Control and

Prevention, said, "Reversing obesity is not going to be done successfully with individual effort."

What is the cause of the modern obesity epidemic?

Biologically, obesity results when the human body persistently takes in, through eating and drinking, more caloric energy than it burns through basic metabolism and muscular exertion. The modern obesity epidemic derives from both an increase in average caloric intake and a decrease in average muscular exertion.

Caloric intake is up. In the United States between 1970 and 2003, average daily caloric intake increased 23 percent to a level of 2,757 calories, roughly 20 percent more than the World Health Organization recommends. Meanwhile, average muscular exertion has declined, as travel takes place less often on foot and more often by car and as physical demands in both the home and the workplace have been reduced. In the home, cleaning floors and washing clothing or dishes are now electrically powered. The removal of snow, the cutting of grass, and the trimming of hedges have been motorized. Washing automobiles is now automated, and seasonal chores such as hanging storm windows no longer exist. Stair climbing has been replaced by elevators, and physical labors both on the farm and in the factory have been replaced by sedentary white-collar work behind a desk in the office.

Despite a booming fitness industry, working out has declined as commuting time has lengthened and as more leisure time is spent sitting in front of the home computer. Among American men 40 to 74 years of age, since 1990 the number of people who report exercising three times a week has dropped from

57 percent to 43 percent. Children who once walked to school are now driven, and entertainment after school more often consists of videos, computer games, and texting friends from the comfort of a soft chair. By the late 1990s, the majority of American children watched more than 5 hours of television a day. At school, physical education classes are no longer required or no longer require breaking a sweat. Young people own fancier bicycles but ride them less often.

Does cheap food cause obesity?

Over the course of the 20th century, food became progressively cheaper relative to income. The real cost of food commodities declined by 50 percent thanks to productivity growth on the farm, and average consumer income in the United States increased by roughly 400 percent. Food today is so cheap relative to income that increasing quantities are wasted or simply thrown away. It is partly because food is cheap that personal consumption has increased.

Allegations that farm subsidies have also driven down the price of food are for the most part mistaken. In nearly all rich countries, including the United States, the net effect of farm subsidy policies has been to make food more expensive, usually through import restrictions. Consumers in the European Union pay roughly 42 percent more for agricultural products than they would if the Common Agricultural Policy (CAP) of the European Union did not exist. Consumers in the United States pay roughly 10 percent more, largely due to import restrictions on dairy products, sugar, and peanuts.

It is often alleged, more specifically, that farm subsidy policies in the United States induce obesity by making corn for animal feed artificially cheap, thus lowering the cost of meat and corn-based sweeteners, relative to healthier foods like fruits and vegetables or natural sweeteners. This assertion is also weak. In recent years, the price of corn has been artificially lowered by some government policies (income supports to corn farmers), but at the same time it has been artificially raised by other policies, including a set of import taxes, tax credits, and mandates designed to encourage the use of corn-based ethanol for transport fuel. The price of corn is also driven up by import restrictions on sugar that encourage the use of corn-based sweeteners such as high-fructose corn syrup (HFCS). In addition, corn subsidy policies do not drive red meat consumption. Per capita beef consumption in the United States peaked in 1976, when farm subsidy policies on balance were making corn artificially expensive. It is not because corn is cheap that America has an obesity crisis; Europe, where farm policy has made corn artificially expensive, also has an obesity crisis.

The charge that junk-food prices have fallen while fruit and vegetable prices have not is also bogus. A 2008 study by the Economic Research Service at the U.S. Department of Agriculture shows that over the past 25 years the price of fruit and vegetable products in the marketplace (controlling for quality and season of the year) fell at almost exactly the same rate as the price of chocolate chip cookies, cola, ice cream, and potato chips. The price of traditional in-season fruit and vegetable products has fallen, and the variety and year-round availability of these products have dramatically increased. Americans are not more obese because healthy foods have become less available. American supermarkets today carry as many as 400 different produce items, up from an average of just 150 different items in the 1970s.

Do fast foods, junk foods, prepared foods, and sweetened beverages cause obesity?

Yes, they do. Four new sources of calorie intake entered the American diet in the final decades of the 20th century: super-sized fast foods, energy-dense snack foods, ready-made prepared foods, and sweetened juice beverages. Increased consumption of these products explains much of the obesity crisis in America today. It is not unusual for an individual meal at a fast-food restaurant to contain more than 1,000 calories. Potato chips contain 155 calories *per ounce*. It would take 18 minutes of jogging to burn off this much energy. Careful studies that control for variables such as income, education, and race have shown that obesity rates among ninth grade schoolchildren are 5 percent higher if the school is located within one-tenth of a mile of a fast-food outlet. The National Restaurant Association rejects such studies as "slapdash," yet local political pressures are rising to zone fast-food restaurants away from public schools. Fast-food chains have responded with significant menu changes. Burger King announced in 2009 three new kids meals that included smaller burgers, sliced applies designed to look like french fries, reduced-sodium chicken tenders, and fat-free chocolate milk. McDonald's now offers apples and yogurt.

The single largest driver of the obesity epidemic may be sweetened beverages. The average American today gets more than 450 calories a day from beverages, including juices, dairy drinks, sweetened soft drinks, and alcohol. Beverages provide twice as many calories today as they did in 1965, with more than two-thirds of the increase coming from sweetened fruit juices and soft drinks. Specialists calculate that the current epidemic of obesity can be accounted for by the consumption of a single extra 20-ounce soft drink each day. It is often alleged that the sweetening of beverages with HFCS rather than natural sugar makes drinks more obesity inducing, but the evidence to support this charge is weak. High-fructose corn syrup in soft drinks consists of 55 percent fructose and 45 percent glucose, not significantly different from ordinary sugar, which is 50 percent fructose and 50 percent glucose. Michael Jacobson, director of the Center for Science and the Public Interest, says the popular idea that HFCS carries a greater obesity risk is "an urban myth."

Is the food industry to blame for the way we eat?

Yes, to some extent. The modern food industry does more than simply process, package, and deliver foods to consumers. It designs foods, often manipulating the ingredients, including the sugar, fat, and salt content, to make them more difficult for consumers to resist. Dr. David Kessler, a former head of the U.S. Food and Drug Administration, charged in 2009 that modern food companies are in part to blame for our overeating because they design foods for irresistibility, delivering tastes and textures that hit an intentionally addictive "bliss point."

Whatever the reason, diet quality in the United States has deteriorated even as caloric quantity has increased. Over the past two decades, the share of Americans age 40 to 74 who eat five servings of fruits and vegetables a day has dropped from 42 percent to 26 percent. Multiple factors have driven this outcome, including the entry of more women into the formal workforce, resulting in fewer home-prepared meals, a rapidly growing preference for meals that can be held in one hand for eating in the car while commuting, the greater leisure time spent today snacking while watching television, and less cigarette smoking, which often leads to more eating. The food industry, represented politically in the United States through the Grocery Manufacturers Association (GMA), attempts to present itself as a guardian of consumer health and well-being that is "committed to helping arrest and reverse the growth of obesity around the world." Yet it is telling that the GMA does not favor governmental regulation of the caloric content of foods or beverages, instead calling for "consumer education," even though there are known limits to what consumers are willing to learn. One government survey of consumer use of nutrition labels on food packages in 2005–6 found that fewer shoppers (only 39 percent) read the nutrition labels "always or often" compared to 10 years earlier.

Up to a point, food companies can be induced to change their behavior without direct regulation. In 2005, the U.S. Department of Health and Human Services jointly with the Department of Agriculture published new *Dietary Guidelines for Americans* that recommended half of daily grain intake should come from whole grains. In response, bread companies voluntarily reformulated products so they could claim a higher whole grain content, yet some then defeated the purpose by making the reformulation more palatable with added quantities of sugar, salt, or fat. In 2006, the Food and Drug Administration began to require disclosure of trans fat content on food labels, and New York City banned trans fats in restaurant foods. This experience induced a number of food manufacturers, including Nestlé, Kraft, Campbell's, Kellogg's, and Frito-Lay, to reformulate products to eliminate trans fats entirely, and several major food service companies, including McDonald's and Burger King, announced their intent to begin using frying oils with no trans fats. Kentucky

Fried Chicken began replacing trans fats early in anticipation of the New York City ban.

Yet the switch to healthy foods is not always good for health because many consumers eat these foods in excessive quantities, responding to what is called the "halo effect." Consumers who might have eaten two regular cookies decide to eat five no-trans-fat cookies. Other consumers are simply not attracted to the healthier choices. When the Dannon company reduced the sugar content in its product lines, it did so without telling customers for fear some would feel they were no longer getting "their money's worth."

A leading supermarket operator in the United States, Delhaize America, is now promoting a system called Guiding Stars, which rates the nutritional value of most of the food and beverage products sold in their stores (it is revealing that 72 percent of the products for sale receive no stars at all). Customer purchases in these supermarkets have shifted significantly toward the products that do have stars. Yet the political power of the food industry blocks any move to make such a system mandatory. The American Beverage Association, through its friends on the Senate and House Agricultural Committees, was able to ensure that federal guidelines for high school lunch programs placed no restrictions at all on sugared soft drinks, sports drinks, caffeinated beverages, sweet fruit juice, or sugar-sweetened milk containing 50 percent more calories than soft drinks.

All postindustrial societies are seeing a strong trend away from diets based on traditional foods prepared at home. In the United States, as of 1997, roughly 40 percent of all food expenditures went for meals prepared by others (either restaurant meals or store-bought prepared meals) rather than at home. When meals are taken in isolation or away from the home, irresponsible food and beverage intake increases. Throughout Europe, a rapid increase in the number of women in the workforce has undercut traditional at-home meal preparation there as well, creating a parallel shift toward the consumption of high-calorie fast foods and convenience foods. In the United Kingdom, 27 percent of all food spending is now for meals from outside the home, and in Spain, 26 percent. In France, time spent on meal preparation at home has fallen by half since the 1960s, and fast-food restaurants are on the rise even in Greece and Portugal. The much-praised Mediterranean diet (based on vegetables, fruit, unrefined grains, and olive oil) is now disappearing even from Mediterranean countries. As fast-food chains have spread in Greece, three-quarters of the adult population has become overweight or obese, an even higher rate than in the United States. Between 1982 and 2002, the percentage of overweight boys in Greece increased by more than 200 percent, and the increase has continued since then. Italy and Spain are not far behind, with more than 50 percent of adults now overweight.

What government actions are being taken to reverse the obesity epidemic?

Governments have so far done little to reverse the obesity crisis. In part, this can be traced to a surprising acceptance of the trend in the minds of those who suffer from the problem. Close to half of those who are obese in America say their body weight is not an issue, and more than 40 percent of parents with obese children describe their child as being "about the right weight." The social normalization of obesity is even promoted by civil rights advocates for the overweight, led in the United States by the National Association to Advance Fat Acceptance (NAAFA), an organization that has been operating since 1969.

An NGO calling itself the International Size Acceptance Association (ISAA) fights discrimination against the overweight around the world.

In elite professional circles in the United States and in Europe, obesity does carry a heavy stigma, raising the possibility that excessive calorie consumption may eventually be brought under control in much the same way cigarette smoking was reduced—through social pressure. On the other hand, the social and political parallels between tobacco use and calorie intake are actually quite weak. Individuals are able to set a personal goal of quitting smoking completely, something they cannot do for eating. Smoking bans in public places make health sense, but eating bans do not. There is no secondhand health risk to sitting next to an overeater. Cigarettes and alcohol can be heavily taxed as "sins," but heavy taxes on food would be considered unjust to the poor and rejected.

Despite such differences, proposals are nonetheless made to use the power of the state to engineer a social reduction in calorie intake, starting with public school lunch meals. Schools and school boards are now cutting lunchroom portions, limiting the snack foods and beverages sold through vending machines, and even restricting what parents are allowed to send to school with their children. Currently, from 500 to 600 school districts across the country have policies that limit the amount of fat, trans fat, sodium, and sugar in food sold or served at school. In California since 2005, state lawmakers have required that snacks sold during the school day contain no more than 35 percent sugar by weight and derive no more than 35 percent of their calories from fat. In Piedmont, California, the high school even banned traditional fund-raising bake sales.

Other countries go further. In France since 2004, the government has begun to operate a Let's Prevent Obesity in Children program under which children from 5 to 12 years old are weighed and their BMI calculated annually, with a letter to their parents reporting and explaining the result. In Brazil and in Mexico, requirements are in place to move school meals toward healthier selections and end the use of whole milk in poverty programs. Much more can be done by employing the taxing and regulatory power of the state. In New York City beginning in 2008, restaurant chains were obliged to post the calorie count of the dishes they serve. Regulatory power could also be used to restrict portion size in fast-food restaurants, tax the added sugar in beverages, or tax the fat in milk. The revenues from such taxes could go to nutrition education and fitness programs. Bans on advertising foods to children could be imposed, and more stringent labeling rules regarding the caloric content of complete food packages (not just individual servings) could be set in place.

Obesity action groups advocate such interventions, but the food and beverage industry resists by invoking the rights of individual customers to make their own calorie intake decisions. Kevin Keane, a spokesperson for the American Beverage Association, said in 2009, "It's overreaching when government uses the tax code to tell people what they can eat or drink." Some segments of society even profit from obesity. One such segment is the $50 billion annual diet and exercise industry. Pharmaceutical and medical companies that sell treatments (not cures) for those who develop type 2 diabetes, high blood pressure, and high cholesterol are also making money from the crisis. In 2004, the federal Medicare program in the United States determined that obesity could be considered a disease, which brought under coverage a new range of expensive diet programs, surgeries, and services such as behavioral and psychological counseling. Heavy lobbying for this decision came from the American Obesity Association (AOA), an advocacy group that wants increased medical care for overweight people funded by insurance companies and taxpayers but stops short of calling for tighter regulations or higher taxes on food and beverage industries.

9

THE POLITICS OF FARM SUBSIDIES AND TRADE

Do all governments give subsidies to farmers?

The governments of nearly all rich countries provide subsidies to support the income of farmers. In 2006, according to calculations by the Organization for Economic Co-operation and Development (OECD), government policies in these rich countries transferred $283 billion worth of income to farmers either through trade interventions (e.g., tariffs or export subsidies) to boost internal farm prices, through public spending to purchase farm commodities (for storage, for domestic Food Stamp programs, or for foreign food aid), or through direct cash transfers. Roughly 29 percent of all farm earnings in these countries depended on such government programs.

Levels of dependence on government support differ significantly country by country; those with the least agricultural potential usually feature the highest levels of support. In alpine Switzerland, where agriculture contributes less than 1 percent to gross domestic product (GDP), 68 percent of all farm income is derived from government supports. In the European Union, the portion is 32 percent; in the United States, it is 16 percent; and in Australia, it is just 5 percent. In New Zealand, where agriculture still makes up 6 percent of

GDP and provides half of all export receipts, farmers depend on the government for only 1 percent of their income. Levels of dependence also vary by commodity. Farmers who produce exported goods normally get less support than farmers who produce goods that compete with imports.

Governments in poor developing countries provide much less subsidy support to agriculture despite being far more "agricultural." In fact, poor countries often make a practice of taxing their farmers to help finance subsidies for urban food consumers. They rig their internal markets to oblige farmers to sell food at an artificially low price, thus creating an income transfer away from farmers and toward food consumers. So while policies in rich countries tend to be rural biased, policies in poor countries tend to be urban biased.

What explains the tendency of rich countries to subsidize farmers?

Governments usually start subsidizing farmers during initial industrial development. All economic sectors become wealthier in this industrialization process, including the farming sector, but the owners and operators of less competitive farms feel themselves losing from the process because more of their fellow citizens begin to earn even higher wages off the farm in the growing industrial sector. And within their own sector, larger and more competitive farms begin buying up small farms to take full advantage of newly available powered machinery such as tractors and harvesting combines. Small farmers see their neighbors and their own children leave farming to take city jobs. Confronting such changes, traditional farmers decide for cultural as well as economic reasons to organize and seek income support from their government. Feeling that they are losing out in the economic marketplace, they form lobby groups and take action in the political marketplace, demanding income support through import restrictions, government price guarantees, tax breaks and subsidized loans, or direct cash payments.

The countries of Europe were the first to industrialize, so they were also the first to begin providing subsidies to farmers, especially during and after World War I. The United States began regulating agricultural markets and providing subsidy benefits to farmers a bit later, during the Great Depression of the 1930s with the enactment of the Agricultural Adjustment Act (AAA) in 1933, as part of President Franklin D. Roosevelt's New Deal program. Agricultural subsidy policies were embraced still later by Japan, when that nation moved toward full industrial development in the 1950s and 1960s, and still later in Taiwan and South Korea, when rapid industrial growth reached those countries in the 1970s and 1980s.

The remarkable uniformity of this farm subsidy response to rapid industrial development has been measured by economists. One comparative study of protection offered to farm sectors across the industrial world found that 60 to 70 percent of all variations in protection levels could be explained solely through reference to the comparative advantage that the agricultural sector had lost relative to the industrial sector.

Do farmers in rich countries need subsidies to survive?

When farm subsidies were initiated in the United States in 1933, most farmers were relatively poor, with an average income less than half that of nonfarmers. At this point in the depths of the Great Depression, subsidies to farmers had economic and social justification. This justification diminished, however, during and after World War II, when millions of farmers left the land to take higher paying jobs in urban industry, resulting in a consolidation of farms into much larger and far more prosperous production units, most of which no longer needed subsidies to survive and prosper. Thanks to farm consolidations, the greatest share of all food production in America today comes from large commercial farmers with an average income level higher than that of most nonfarmers, and an average net worth much higher because of the valuable land, buildings, and machinery they own. By 1995, roughly 90 percent of all farm commodities produced in the United States were by farmers with at least 1,800 acres of land and a net worth of at least $600,000.

These large commercial farmers do not need subsidies to remain more prosperous than most of their fellow citizens, yet they continue to get the largest share of the subsidies. Farm subsidies, typically linked to production volume, are almost never targeted to small farmers or to those in greatest need. In the United States in one recent year, the largest 7 percent of farms got 45 percent of all agricultural subsidies. In Europe, the wealthiest 20 percent of farmers receive more than 80 percent of the subsidies.

Political efforts to improve the targeting of subsidy payments are routinely blocked by the entrenched farm lobby. In 2008, President George W. Bush proposed to Congress that the law should be changed to prevent the delivery of subsidy payments to farmers who earned more than $200,000, but the Senate voted that the cap should be set instead at $750,000, and the House of Representatives then said there should be no cap at all. In the final measure that passed, a $750,000 income limit was set for receiving some direct payments, but other payments continued to go out no matter how much a farmer already earned. Farmers can evade even the $750,000 limit by dividing the reported income of their operation between themselves and their spouse.

Why don't taxpayers and food consumers join to resist farm subsidies?

As industrial development advances, farm subsidy policies can become costly both to taxpayers and food consumers. By the middle years of the 1980s in the United States, farm subsidies were costing ordinary citizens $30 billion a year as taxpayers and an additional $6 billion as food consumers. In the European Community that year, taxpayer costs were $16 billion, and consumer costs were $33 billion. In Japan, taxpayer costs were $6 billion, and consumer costs were $28 billion. Consumer costs are larger in Europe and Japan because the income transfer to farmers is accomplished more through food import restrictions, which drive up the prices paid by consumers.

Consumers and taxpayers seldom make serious demands to reduce farm subsidies because it is easier for farmers to organize politically to defend subsidies than for taxpayers and consumers to organize to attack them. This fits a well-established rule originally supplied by economist Mancur Olson that smaller groups are easier to organize than larger groups because the individual share of any benefit secured will be greater and because it is easier for small groups to discipline free-riding noncontributors. Some studies of farm subsidies even show that smaller commodity groups (e.g., sugar farmers) do better than larger groups in securing subsidy benefits. Also, as the total number of farmers shrinks under industrial development, the average benefit per farmer can go up dramatically without generating a higher cost overall. Furthermore, when total subsidy costs do increase, it is scarcely noticed by consumers and taxpayers because consumer income gains and gains from higher farm productivity have reduced the average share of American income spent on food from 41 percent a century ago to just 10 percent today. The drop would have been a bit deeper without farm subsidies, but consumers can be happy either way. As for taxpayers, because federal spending overall has grown more rapidly than farm subsidy spending, the salience of farm subsidy spending continues to decline. The federal government spends more now on food stamps for consumers than it spends on subsidies for farmers.

What is the farm bill and what is the farm lobby?

The legislative package that renews America's farm subsidy entitlement system every 5 years or so is known as the *farm bill*, and the organized groups that promote the bill are known as the *farm lobby*. The most recent farm bill enacted in 2008 carried a 5-year price tag of $286 billion. President George W. Bush was not running for reelection, so he dared to veto the bill, calling it wasteful. Congress, however, reenacted the same bill over the president's veto, passing it by wide margins of 316–108 in the House and 82–13 in the Senate. Many knew that bill was wasteful but opted to vote for it anyway so as not to anger the farm lobby in an election year.

The secret to every farm bill's success in Congress is the lead role played by the House and Senate Agriculture Committees, where members from farm states and farm districts enjoy a dominant presence and are rewarded for their legislative efforts with generous campaign contributions from the farm lobby, which is built around organizations representing the farmers who get the subsidies. The Agriculture Committees draft the legislation that goes to the floor for a final vote, and in the drafting process they take care to satisfy the minimum needs of both Republican and Democratic members to ensure bipartisan support. For example, the farm bill enacted in 2002 emerged from the House Agriculture Committee without a single dissenting vote. The drafters also give generous treatment both to northern crops and southern crops, and they take care to attach generous funding for domestic food and nutrition programs (like Food Stamps) to lock in support from urban district members. Then they add some measures to please environmentalists, such as a Conservation Reserve Program (CRP) that pays farmers to leave their land (temporarily) idle. The final package is what students of legislative politics call a committee-based logroll.

When the farm bill leaves the committees and reaches the floor, another classic legislative mechanism pushes it toward enactment: vote trading. Farm district members implicitly or explicitly promise support on multiple measures of future interest to urban and suburban members in return for their single "aye" vote on the farm bill once every 5 years. These trades always bring in enough nonfarm support to ensure a majority.

This farm subsidy renewal process is supported by a formidable nexus of institutions often referred to as an *iron triangle*. At the congressional corner of the triangle are the House and Senate Agriculture Committees, populated and often chaired by strong farm subsidy advocates. At the executive corner is the U.S. Department of Agriculture (USDA), which administers the subsidy programs and values them as a way to protect the department from irrelevance in a postagricultural age. At the third corner are the private farm lobby organizations. The best known of these are two general farm organizations. The American Farm Bureau Federation (commonly known as the Farm Bureau) represents the interests of large commercial farmers, mostly Republicans. The National Farmers Union (NFU) represents the interests of smaller farmers, mostly Democrats. When it comes to shaping the details of the farm bill, the most influential private lobby organizations are those representing individual commodity producer groups, such as the National Corn Growers Association, the U.S. Wheat Associates, the National Cotton Council of America, or the National Milk Producers Federation. These organizations contribute generously to the reelection campaigns of their favorite Agriculture Committee members, and they send experienced and always affable operatives to work the halls and committee rooms of Congress during the legislative drafting process.

The continuing clout of the farm lobby is visible in the astonishing outcome of the 2008 farm bill debate, which took place when America's farmers were enjoying unprecedented prosperity thanks to the highest market prices for farm commodities in more than three decades. Net farm income in 2008 reached $89 billion, 40 percent above the average of the previous 10 years. Yet without any sense of irony or shame, the farm lobby asserted that America's farmers were facing "emergencies" of various kinds and needed new "safety nets" for protection. The new measure pushed through was an Average Crop Revenue Election (ACRE) program that cleverly used the high income levels of 2008 as a baseline from which farmers would be able to make claims for added compensation in the event prices subsequently fell, which of course they soon did. The 2008 bill also included new funding for nutrition programs, research on organic agriculture and specialty crops, conservation measures, and block grants to promote horticultural products. There was something for everybody, making passage over the president's veto a certainty.

Why does the government subsidize ethanol?

Outside the farm bill process, Congress since the 1970s has also enacted subsidies to promote the use of corn to produce ethanol, a product that can be blended with gasoline to make *gasohol* and used as an automobile fuel. Currently, the government provides a 45 cents per gallon tax credit (about $3 billion a year) to the industries that blend ethanol with gasoline, while imposing a 54 cents per gallon duty at the border to block the import of sugar-based ethanol from Brazil and the Caribbean. In addition, the Energy Independence and Security Act of 2007 mandated a "renewable fuel standard" requiring that by 2015 the United States will be using 15 billion gallons of conventional biofuels such as corn-based ethanol—implying a significant increase from the 2009 level of approximately 11 billion gallons.

Promoting corn-based ethanol is sometimes depicted as a path to energy independence because it reduces the need to import foreign oil to make gasoline. It is also depicted as a path to environmental sustainability because biofuels are renewable, unlike gasoline that comes from petroleum. On closer examination, both arguments are weak. Even if the current ethanol program were scaled up dramatically, it would gain only a small measure of energy independence for the United States. Currently, the United States uses less than one-third of its corn crop for ethanol production; even if it were to devote all of its corn production to fuel use (which nobody would dare propose), consumption of gasoline would decline by only 13 percent, scarcely reducing total oil import requirements.

The environmental benefits of corn-based ethanol are equally dubious. Ethanol from corn may be renewable, but it is neither cheap nor clean. If it were really cheap, it would not need government subsidies to survive, and the manufacture of ethanol causes significant pollution. A 2008 study in the journal *Science* concluded that if worldwide land use changes are taken into account, the greenhouse gas emissions from first producing and then burning corn-based ethanol would exceed those from producing and burning gasoline. It makes greater environmental sense, as well as greater commercial sense, to burn ethanol produced from sugar rather than corn, yet the American government does not allow that to happen; it keeps sugar-based ethanol out of the domestic market with an import duty.

The success of the corn-based ethanol lobby in part reflects the fact that every 4 years America's aspiring presidential candidates compete in early party caucuses in Iowa, the nation's leading corn and ethanol state. It is not possible to do well in these caucuses without endorsing subsidies, import protections, and production mandates for corn-based ethanol.

How do farm subsidies shape international agricultural trade?

The farm subsidies operating in nearly all rich countries have long tended to distort production and trade. They cause too much food to be produced in regions not well suited to farming, such as alpine countries in Europe, desert lands in the American southwest, or the municipal suburbs of Japan, and too little to be produced in the developing countries of the tropics where agricultural potential is often far more bountiful. Farm subsidies in Europe, the United States, and Japan also take market share away from some rich countries such as Australia and New Zealand that are far better suited to some kinds of farming. Sugar markets are one example. Because of guarantees of high sugar prices engineered through import restrictions in Europe and the United States, too much of the world's sugar production comes from the growing of sugar beets inside these two markets rather than from cane sugar in the Caribbean, Brazil, or tropical Africa. By one respected calculation, protectionist farm subsidy policies cause at least 40 percent of the world's sugar to be grown in the wrong place.

The damages done by the farm policies of rich countries to farmers in poor countries can be quantified. In a formal complaint brought against American cotton subsidies in 2002, the government of Brazil showed that without government subsidies cotton production in the United States would have been 29 percent lower and cotton exports from the United States would have been 41 percent lower—and international cotton prices would have been boosted by 13 percent. The elimination of such subsidies would benefit cotton farmers in Africa as well as in Brazil. For many poor families in West Africa who live on less than $1 a day per person, cotton sales are the only source of cash income. According to calculations done by Oxfam America, if U.S. cotton programs were eliminated and if the international price of cotton consequently increased by 6 to 14 percent, eight very poor countries in West Africa would be able to earn an additional $191 million each year in foreign exchange from their cotton exports, and household income in these countries would increase by 2.3 to 5.7 percent.

Why hasn't the WTO been able to discipline farm subsidies?

Many farm subsidy policies distort international trade either by stimulating excessive production, and hence exports, or by blocking imports. One purpose of the World Trade Organization (WTO) is to reduce such trade distortions, yet successive rounds of multilateral trade negotiations in the WTO (and within its predecessor organization, the General Agreement on Tariffs and Trade, or GATT) have failed to make more than modest progress in achieving this goal. As of 2008, the average tariff applied to agricultural imports around the world (calculated from the vantage point of U.S. exporters) was nearly 17 percent, three times the average tariff on manufactured goods. In some of the largest and most lucrative markets, the average tariff is even higher. Agricultural products of the United States entering the European Union encounter an average tariff of 30 percent, and American farm sales to Japan encounter a 59 percent average tariff.

Barriers to international agricultural trade are difficult to bring down because without import barriers, domestic farm support policies would be far more expensive for governments to operate, especially in Europe and Japan. It is politically easy to transfer income to farmers through import restrictions because they do not cost anything in budget terms (they may actually earn government revenues) and because they push some of their costs onto foreign producers (who do not vote). The agricultural trade policies of the United States would probably be just as reliant on such import restrictions if America's farmers were less productive and hence more vulnerable to foreign competition.

In the rounds of international agricultural trade negotiations that take place periodically within the WTO, a distinction is drawn between subsidies to farmers that distort production (and hence, trade) versus those that do not. The current strategy is to negotiate limits on trade-distorting subsidies only, allowing governments to provide farmers with as many cash subsidies as they wish as long as the payments are "decoupled" from any incentive to produce more. Payments that supposedly do not incentivize new production are placed in a so-called green box, while policies that clearly distort production are placed either in a red box (they are banned) or in an amber box (where they are allowed, but only up to a certain dollar value). Since the completion of the Uruguay Round of multilateral negotiations in 1994, the European Union has partly decoupled a larger portion of its farm income support policies, allowing them to fall into a so-called blue box.

Even with these various green box and blue box exemptions, it proved impossible to reach an agreement on new amber box disciplines in the most recent Doha Round of WTO negotiations, initiated in 2001. In July 2008, U.S. Trade Representative Susan Schwab offered to place a $15 billion cap on trade-distorting amber box U.S. farm subsidies, an offer later lowered to $14.5 billion in hopes of gaining acceptance from Brazil. Schwab was able to make such an offer in 2008 only because high commodity prices temporarily reduced the value of America's trade-distorting subsidies to a level well below $14.5 billion, which diminished the chances the farm lobby would object. Also, the offer was contingent on an equally significant offer from the European Union, and it was well known that the European Union wanted no new disciplines on trade-distorting subsidies beyond cuts it had already made unilaterally. The talks collapsed without a result when some developing countries—led by China—concluded that the new access they might gain to agricultural markets in the United States and European Union envisioned under the proposals then on the table was not enough to justify the added access they would have to provide to their own domestic markets for agricultural and manufacturing goods.

Did NAFTA hurt poor corn farmers in Mexico?

Because multilateral negotiations so frequently stall, the United States in recent decades has attempted to open markets abroad through bilateral or regional trade agreements, beginning with the North American Free Trade Agreement (NAFTA) completed in 1993. This agreement triggered a significant phase out of agricultural import barriers between the United States and Mexico, but it was opposed by antiglobalization advocacy groups such as the Institute for Agriculture and Trade Policy (IATP) in Minneapolis. They argued that the agreement would hurt poor corn farmers in Mexico by exposing them to a flood of cheap imports of corn from subsidized growers in the United States. This would push millions off the land and into urban slums, contributing eventually to larger flows of both legal and illegal Mexican immigrants to the United States.

Reviewing actual experience since 1993, Mexico did import much more corn from the United States after NAFTA, but this was mostly yellow corn for animal feed to support expanding hog and poultry production, not the white corn grown by poor farmers in Mexico for tortillas. Corn production inside Mexico itself continued to increase despite higher imports, in part because commercial corn growers in Mexico were also getting subsidies (37 percent of the income of Mexican corn growers came from government supports in 2002 compared to 26 percent in the United States). Poor growers of white corn are leaving the land in Mexico, but they are noncompetitive because of their own deficits in technology and infrastructure caused by decades of neglect from their own government more than because of diminished trade protection at the border. Mexico's overall agricultural trade balance has improved under NAFTA, as agricultural exports (high-value fruits and vegetables) grew by 9.4 percent between 1994 and 2001, while agricultural imports increased by only 6.9 percent. The price of corn did fall inside Mexico under NAFTA, but this lower price provided significant gains for the urban poor who rely on a corn-based diet, a fact dramatized when a temporary increase in corn prices in 2007 prompted poor consumers in Mexico City to stage a mass protest.

This Mexican case underscores an important point. The welfare of food producers and food consumers usually depends more on what governments do inside the border than on what they do with their trade policy at the border. Arguments between open trade advocates and trade protectionists too often miss this point.

10

AGRICULTURE, THE ENVIRONMENT, AND FARM ANIMALS

How does farming damage the environment?

From a pure ecology perspective, all forms of agriculture damage the natural environment. When our distant ancestors went from hunting and gathering to planting crops and grazing animals, forests were cut and waterways were redirected. Plants and animals were domesticated and progressively modified through selective breeding. Using a more socially centered or utilitarian perspective, such modifications to nature will be considered damage only if they bring long-term costs to human society that exceed the short-term food production gain. Many kinds of farming are environmentally costly even within this narrow definition.

It is useful to classify the environmental damage done by farming according to where the damage takes place: on the farm versus off the farm. Farmers themselves suffer most from damage on the farm. Nonfarmers suffer most if the damage is off the farm or downstream. Politics often sets the balance between these two kinds of damage. Farmers in poor countries lack political power, so they often find themselves trapped into practices that damage their own farm resource base and hence their own livelihood. Farmers in rich countries, because they have abundant political power, often use that power to push the environmental damage they do onto nonfarmers.

In the poorest developing countries, nearly all of the environmental damage done by agriculture takes place on the farm. Prime examples include the exhaustion of soil nutrients due to shortened fallow times and inadequate fertilizer use, waterlogging of soils due to mismanaged irrigation, and the *desertification* of rangeland caused by mismanaged animal grazing. By harming the agricultural resource base itself, this sort of damage helps keep farmers poor. The shortening of fallow times in Africa is now removing nitrogen from the soil at an average annual rate of 22–26 kilograms per hectare, too much to be offset by current rates of fertilizer application, which average only 9 kilograms per hectare. The result of this "soil mining" is a deficit in soil nutrients that causes annual crop losses estimated at between $1 billion and $3 billion. This is not the end of the problem. As cultivated soils become exhausted, farmers extend cropping onto new lands, cutting more trees and destroying more wildlife habitat. Land clearing for the expansion of unsustainable low-yield farming causes roughly 70 percent of all deforestation in Africa.

In the agricultural systems of wealthy industrial societies, by contrast, environmental damage from farming usually results from too much input use rather than too little, and those who suffer most are usually not farmers. For example, excessive nitrogen fertilizer use leads to nitrate runoff and downstream eutrophication of streams and ponds. In Europe, excess nitrates in water supplies are a downstream health hazard (blue baby syndrome). In the United States, excessive nitrogen fertilizer use on farms along the Mississippi River watershed has contributed to an environmental calamity both within the watershed itself and in the Gulf of Mexico where an expanding "dead zone" is no longer able to support aquatic life. In a similar manner, excessive diversion of surface water for crop irrigation leads to shortages downstream for residential or industrial use—a serious problem in California. Concentrated animal feeding operations (CAFOs) designed to cut livestock industry costs by fattening thousands of animals for slaughter all within one crowded facility pollute both the air and water with toxic effluents, creating health risks for nonfarming human populations living nearby.

What kind of farming is environmentally sustainable?

Environmental activists and agricultural scientists answer this question in dramatically different ways. Environmentalists prefer small-scale diversified farming systems that rely on fewer inputs purchased off the farm, systems that imitate nature rather than seek to dominate nature. Agricultural scientists often believe there will be less harm done to nature overall by highly capitalized and specialized high-yield farming systems employing the latest technology. Increasing the yield on lands already farmed allows more of the remaining land to be saved for nature. Environmentalists invoke the damage done by modern farming, whereas agricultural scientists invoke the greater damage that would be done if the same production volume had to come from less productive low-yield farming systems.

The environmentalist side of this argument was most eloquently laid out in 1962 in Rachel Carson's landmark book, *Silent Spring*, which exposed the damage done by chemical pesticides both to human health and to wild animal species (including songbirds, hence the title). Carson's book led both to a specific ban on the production of DDT in America and to the formation of a broad and powerful national environmental movement that secured passage of the National Environmental Protection Act in 1970. This act created America's Environmental Protection Agency (EPA). Carson's thinking also triggered an enduring quest among environmentalists for alternatives to high-yield, high-input farming.

One early pioneer in this search for alternative models of farming was Wes Jackson, who founded a Land Institute in Kansas in 1976 to promote a model of farming based on polycultures of perennial crops rather than monocultures of annual crops. This particular model did not emerge as a commercial success, but it was Jackson, in 1980, who began employing the term *sustainable agriculture* to describe his objective. Responding to demands for an alternative approach, the Department of Agriculture in 1985 finally initiated a program to promote what was then called low-impact sustainable agriculture (LISA). Conventional commercial farmers panned it as "low-income sustainable agriculture," but the idea gained traction both with nonfarming urban elites and with a younger cohort of small farmers linked to a countercultural back-to-the-land movement from the 1960s.

High-input farming did cause environmental damage in America during the second half of the 20th century, but the earlier style of low-input farming had been damaging as well. It was an extension of low-yield wheat farming into the southern plains of Kansas, Oklahoma, and the Texas panhandle in the 1920s—before synthetic chemical fertilizers or pesticides were in wide use—that produced America's single greatest environmental disaster up until then, a drought-induced loss of topsoil that ruined farmlands across an area as big as the state of Pennsylvania, turning it into a dust bowl. Roughly 400,000 farmers fled the dust bowl, many of them to California to work as migrants picking tomatoes and peas. This was a flow of environmental refugees that remained unmatched until Hurricane Katrina flooded out the population of New Orleans in 2005.

Following Carson's book, many environmentalists seeking reduced farm chemical use favored a move back in the direction of low-input farming. This was resisted by commercial farmers and agricultural scientists, who remembered the dust bowl and sought ways to contain damage from chemical inputs without abandoning the quest for higher yields. Industry developed chemicals that were less harmful, and farmers found ways to apply them with greater precision, but by that time environmental advocates wanted more than a technical fix. They wanted a more decisive move away from the dominant model of highly capitalized, highly specialized "industrial" farming.

Environmental advocates believe this kind of farming is unsustainable. They agree with the thrust of the 2008 study by the International Assessment of Agricultural Knowledge, Science and Technology for Development (IAASTD), which warned that using still more modern science to "increase yields and productivity" could do even more environmental damage. Growing numbers of popular writers also depict high-yield agriculture as a dead end. In an apocalyptic 2008 book titled *The End of Food*, journalist Paul Roberts argued that the world's large-scale, hyperefficient industrialized food production systems were heading toward an inevitable collapse because of the damage they had been doing to soils, water systems, and other "natural infrastructure." Celebrity food writer Michael Pollan wrote in 2008 that "the era of cheap and abundant food appears to be drawing to a close." Most agricultural specialists take a far less worried view thanks in part to the recent emergence of something called *precision farming*.

What is low-impact or precision farming?

Commercial farming today has moved well beyond the practices Rachel Carson described and justifiably criticized in 1962. Many of the early insecticides then in use have now been banned and replaced by chemicals that are less persistent in the environment and effective when applied in lower volumes. Total chemical use in American agriculture peaked more than 35 years ago in 1973. This deserves to be recognized in part as an important achievement for environmental advocacy, yet one the advocates themselves seldom mention because it could make their current efforts seem less urgent. Soil erosion on farms also dropped sharply thanks to the innovation of *no-till* planting systems later in the 1970s. No-till was originally embraced as a way to reduce the use of diesel fuel during the energy crisis of the 1970s, so it is a method that reduces both fuel use and soil loss on farms.

Innovations that reduced the environmental impact of farming continued in the 1980s and 1990s. Farmers began conserving water through drip irrigation systems and through laser-leveled fields that minimized runoff. Farm tractors acquired satellite-linked Global Positioning System (GPS) monitors and Geographical Information System (GIS) maps that automatically steered their machines (in straighter paths) and told them exactly where they were in a field to within 1 square meter and precisely how much water or fertilizer that part of the field required. Infrared sensors detected the greenness of the crop, telling a farmer exactly how much more (or less) fertilizer might be needed. This is called precision farming. To minimize nitrogen runoff, the fertilizer was inserted in much smaller total quantities at exactly the depth needed and in perfect rows exactly where the plant roots would grow. Eventually, genetically engineered seeds were developed for cotton, corn, and soybean crops that allowed farmers to control pests and weeds with still fewer chemical sprays and still less soil tillage. This led to even less burning of diesel fuel and far more sequestered carbon.

The environmental gains made possible by this movement toward low-impact and precision farming have been considerable. In 2008, the Organization for Economic Co-operation and Development (OECD) in Paris published an important review of the "environmental performance of agriculture" in the 30 most advanced industrial countries of the world (those with the most highly capitalized farming systems). The new data showed that between 1990 and 2004 total food production in these countries increased in volume by 5 percent from an already high level, yet adverse environmental impacts were diminished in nearly every category. The area of land taken up by agriculture declined 4 percent. Soil erosion from both wind and water was reduced. Water use on irrigated lands declined by 9 percent. Energy use on the farm increased at only one-sixth the rate of energy use in the rest of the economy. Gross greenhouse gas emissions from farming fell by 3 percent. Herbicide and insecticide spraying declined by 5 percent. Excessive nitrogen fertilizer use declined by 17 percent. Biodiversity also improved, as increased numbers of crop varieties and livestock breeds came into use.

True believers in precision farming expect there will be no limit to the impact-reducing gains that can be achieved. Their long-term vision includes small solar-powered robots working farm fields in groups, hoeing weeds and picking off bugs

24 hours a day without any polluting chemicals or fossil fuels at all, and then harvesting the crops with almost no human supervision required. Even if this were possible, most environmental advocates would refuse to see it as progress. They generally do not endorse modern precision farming because it favors the highly capitalized industrial-scale model of production they reject. The equipment and training needed to engage in precision farming are beyond the reach of the small farmers that environmentalists prefer to champion. They reject any thought that a biological system such as farming could be sustainably and safely dominated and precision engineered through science. They believe, with Rachel Carson, that nature will always find a way to strike back against human arrogance of this kind.

Do fragile lands, population growth, and poverty make farming unsustainable?

These are popular explanations for environmental damage from farming in poor countries, but institutional variables are usually more important.

The meaning of "fragile" land is elusive. It is true that many poor countries are endowed with less productive farmland resources, such as sloping lands and irregular lands with thin and badly weathered soils, all subject to the damaging extremes of heat, flood, and drought. In many tropical countries, soil nutrients leach away immediately when trees are cut, leaving a baked and barren landscape on which only weeds will grow. Under proper management, however, these less productive tropical lands can be improved dramatically and farmed sustainably. When farmed with adequate fallow time, limed to correct acidity, terraced and mulched to capture and keep more moisture on level soil, or planted with several different crops at the same time (intercropped) to reduce vulnerability to pests, the productive potential of less favored tropical lands does not have to decline.

Some argue that poverty itself is a cause of environmental damage in farming because poor farmers who live from hand to mouth cannot afford to wait for resource-protecting investments to pay off. The weakness in this line of thinking is that many poor farming communities do invest to conserve their resources under the right political and institutional circumstances. They are more than willing to build and maintain terraces, plant trees, and protect rangelands from overgrazing when effective *common property resource* (CPR) systems are allowed to operate at the local or village level. These informal systems protect local forests, streams, ponds, and grazing lands by allocating equitable use to insiders while denying access to outsiders. Such systems are good at blocking the so-called tragedy of the commons, a pattern of environmental destruction that arises in systems of open access (Garrett Hardin, the influential ecologist who named this pattern in 1968, should have called it the tragedy of open access). Within a well-managed commons systems, even poor communities can avoid environmental tragedies.

Commons systems are vulnerable to breakdown, however, if powerful outside institutions such as colonial administrators, international companies, forestry department bureaucrats, megaproject engineers, government land-titling agencies, or centralized irrigation authorities move in to take control away from local community leaders. Local farmers who sense they are about to lose control, but who still have access, will then stop making investments in resource protection. In fact, they will begin using up the resource base as fast as they can—cutting the trees, plowing up terraces, overgrazing the range, over-fishing the ponds—before the outsiders take it away.

Well-functioning common property systems in poor countries can also break down if local leaders become corrupt or if population density increases. With more population, the value per person of protecting the resource will decline on the inside, demotivating efforts at protection just when more outsiders are attempting to gain access. At this point, effective resource protection can require switching to an individual private property system, which turns the problem of excluding outsiders over to the police while restoring individual payoffs to resource-protecting investments. If this transition to individual land ownership is made successfully, a further increase in population density may not threaten the resource base at all. It can make affordable even greater labor investments in protecting the land (mulching, terracing, etc.), and it increases the affordability of investments in rural infrastructure (roads, power, irrigation) to increase the productivity of lands already cultivated, reducing pressures to expand farming onto new lands. One example from Africa is the experience of Machakos District in Kenya, where farmers in this densely settled semiarid area avoided serious damage to their marginal soil endowments even as population increased. This occurred due to clear land ownership that motivated heavier labor investments in terracing systems, the use of more fertilizer, and a shift to higher value crops for sale in nearby urban markets.

Do cash crops and export crops cause environmental harm?

Shifting from food crop production to more specialized cash crop production for export is frequently cited as a cause of both economic dependence and environmental harm. There are some cases that support this generalization. For example, in Central America in the 1960s and 1970s, landlords introduced chemical-intensive cotton production and evicted traditional peasants growing maize and beans. Yet the cash crop versus food crop dichotomy is usually unhelpful because a number of food crops in the developing world are at the same time cash crops (including rice in Asia), and many cash export crops (e.g., cocoa in West Africa) are grown by small farmers in the same fields with food crops in an environmentally friendly intercropping system.

Cash crops grown for export are not inherently less rewarding for small farmers or more damaging to the environment. Exported cash crops are often tree crops or perennials that provide better land cover and more stable root structures than annual food crops. In Africa, some kinds of perennial export crops—such as tea or coffee planted along the contour of sloping lands or oil palm planted in low-lying areas—can protect the soil much better than some food crops (e.g., maize) that require annual tillage. At least a partial switch to higher value cash crops can help farm families with limited land and labor earn the income they need to pay their children's school expenses. Farmers can also switch part of their land to cash crop production and then use the income generated to purchase improved seeds and fertilizer to simultaneously boost food crop production on the rest of their land.

Do farm subsidies promote environmental damage in agriculture?

Yes. Most subsidy policies work by giving farmers artificially high prices for their products, encouraging them to use too many fertilizers and pesticides and too much irrigation water in efforts to boost crop yields as high as possible. In South Korea, where rice farmers are heavily protected (with a guaranteed price roughly five times the world market price), pesticide use is extremely high at 12.8 kilograms per hectare. In France, where farmers have less price protection, pesticide use is less than half as high at 4.5 kilograms per hectare. In the United States, where there is even less protection, pesticide use is only 2.3 kilograms per hectare. And in Senegal, where farmers get almost no protection at all, pesticide use averages only 0.1 kilogram per hectare. In most of Africa, farmers are often taxed rather than subsidized (a symptom of their political weakness), which results in too little input use rather than too much (e.g., not enough fertilizer use to replace depleted soil nutrients).

When subsidies go up, input use often goes up in lockstep. Between 1970 and 1990 in Thailand, as income protections for farmers increased, fertilizer use per hectare increased nearly sevenfold. In Indonesia, the government subsidized fertilizer purchases directly, at one point by as much as 68 percent, so over one 5-year period in the 1980s, fertilizer use increased 77 percent. In India, when the government began to subsidize 86 percent of the electric bill for pumping irrigation water in the Punjab, groundwater tables began dropping at an unsustainable rate of about 0.8 meters a year.

Farmers in rich countries are not only powerful enough politically to demand the subsidies that encourage excessive input use; they are also powerful enough to avoid being held to account for the resulting downstream environmental damage. Because of farm lobby strength, the air and water pollution that emanates from farms in rich countries is regulated far less than pollution from other industries. In the United States, the agricultural sector is significantly exempt from the regulatory structures of both the original Clean Air Act and Clean Water Act. For example, the Environmental Protection Agency (EPA) imposes almost no regulation on air quality at concentrated animal feeding operations (CAFOs) even though they generate 1.6 million tons of manure annually. In 2008, the poultry industry (represented by the National Chicken Council, the U.S. Poultry and Egg Association, and the National Turkey Federation) even secured from EPA a special exemption from simple reporting requirements on ammonia emissions.

Subsidies likewise encourage water pollution. Despite the dead zone in the Gulf of Mexico, Congress does not regulate excess nitrogen runoff from farms and does not tax farm fertilizer use. Instead, it has created voluntary programs that pay farmers to take land (temporarily) out of production or to cultivate their land in ways that reduce runoff. Instead of using the "polluter pays" principle, the government pays the polluter. Even in extreme cases, such as chemical pollution in the Florida Everglades from heavily protected sugar farming, strong regulations are routinely blocked by industry. In 1996, when Vice President Al Gore proposed taxing sugar growers to finance an Everglades cleanup project, a direct phone call from a Florida sugar baron to President Bill Clinton resulted in setting aside the tax proposal.

A more recent example of the power of agriculture to resist environmental regulation in the United States is seen in the case of climate change policy. In 2009, when the House of Representatives passed the Waxman-Markey bill to create a cap-and-trade system to limit greenhouse gas emissions, the entire agricultural sector was left "uncapped." Instead of being subject to caps under this bill, farmers would be entitled to profit by selling "offsets" to industries in sectors that were capped. The offsets would take the form of voluntary reductions in emissions or an increased sequestering of carbon, steps many farmers would be taking anyway.

So far, the only authority strong enough to resist the farm lobby in the United States has been a legal instrument, the nation's 1973 Endangered Species Act. For example, in 2008, a lawsuit filed under that act by the Natural Resources Defense Council forced the Bush administration's Fish and Wildlife Service to divert more than 150 billion gallons of water away from irrigated farming in the San Joaquin Valley in California so as to protect the delta smelt, an endangered 3-inch fish. Environmentalists know that their best chance in a battle against farmers is usually to move the action out of Congress and into the courts.

Is modern farming abusive toward animals?

Vegetarians and vegans believe any human use of animals or animal products for food is abusive and morally wrong. Jeffrey Masson, a former psychoanalyst and Freudian scholar, argues in a 2009 book titled *The Face on Your Plate* that farm animals—even chickens—deserve human respect and should not be killed or used for food. This is a problematic position to take in one respect. Avoiding abuse is important, but if we all became vegans, farm animals would hardly thrive. They are domesticated species that cannot survive without human care, so if we stopped raising them for food, they would have to be kept in zoos or perform in circuses to avoid extinction.

When using farm animals for food, what constitutes respectful and humane treatment? Farm industries, for their own convenience, argue that humane treatment can be measured in terms of the physical health and safety of the animal. The concentrated animal feeding operations used by livestock industries in the United States today often do succeed in minimizing farm animal mortality. Chickens raised in cages encounter fewer health and safety risks from wild birds, insects, and parasites. Animal welfare advocates reject this narrow approach, insisting that humane treatment must also take emotional health into account, requiring that animals be given greater space and freedom to engage in instinctive behaviors. In the case of chickens, this could mean simple behaviors such as foraging for food, perching, and wing flapping. The 95 percent of egg-laying hens in the United States that are confined indoors in cages for their entire lives are unable to engage in such behaviors. The industry even tries to argue that it is humane to cut off part of a chicken's beak (without anesthetic) to prevent cannibalism and feather pecking, but animal welfare advocates assert—with credible evidence—that the practice results in chronic as well as short-term pain. They also say the urge to peck would be reduced in a less crowded or cagefree environment.

At the federal level, farm animal welfare falls under the jurisdiction of the Animal and Plant Health Inspection Service (APHIS) of the U.S. Department of Agriculture, an agency strongly influenced by the livestock industry. Regulations to guarantee the safety of animal products for human consumption are acceptable to industry, but regulations to increase welfare for the animals are routinely opposed. There is federal legislation requiring the humane slaughter of farm animals (the Humane Methods of Slaughter Act) but nothing on humane treatment prior to slaughter other than a "28-hour law" that governs how live farm animals can be transported (they must be given access to food and water at least once every 28 hours, but this law does not extend to poultry). There are federal laws to protect companion animal welfare (the Animal Welfare Act of 1966), but farm animals are excluded, even though some—pigs, for example—have greater intelligence than most household pets.

In the United States, there are two key strategies available to animal welfare advocates. One is to challenge animal abuse indirectly via links to food safety—for example, by exposing slaughterhouses that use meat from sick and mistreated animals (e.g., cattle unable to stand up). The second strategy has been to seek stronger welfare protections directly but at the state level through ballot initiatives. In California in 2008, a coalition of farm animal welfare advocates succeeded in passing Proposition 2, a ballot initiative that requires all egg producers, by the year 2015, to house their hens in spaces large enough for them to stand up and turn around. The initiative passed by a 63 percent vote following an emotional battle between supporters (who broadcast video footage of miserable-looking animals cramped inside dark, filthy cages) and industry opponents (who warned of higher food prices). Together, the opposing sides spent nearly $16 million on the campaign.

Because the humane treatment of farm animals is more expensive for industry, it is unlikely ever to be undertaken spontaneously. Building a cagefree facility for egg-laying hens costs about three times as much per bird as conventional battery cages. Europe has used direct regulation to overcome industry resistance, with rules for pig farmers that require less cramped and monotonous conditions, but industry in Europe had not yet gone so far down the CAFO road, so this was more easily accomplished there. In the United States, other than through direct regulation, an alternative means to promote farm animal welfare is through private standards imposed on livestock industries by the food companies and restaurants that purchase animal products in bulk. The McDonald's Corporation has established welfare guidelines for egg-laying hens that require a minimum cage space of 75 square centimeters, imposing slightly higher costs on its suppliers. For wealthy societies, the slightly higher costs (roughly 9–12 cents per dozen eggs) are easily affordable.

11

AGRIBUSINESS, SUPERMARKETS, AND FAST FOOD

What does the word agribusiness mean?

The term *agribusiness* was coined in 1957 by two professors at the Harvard Business School, Ray Goldberg and John H. Davis, in recognition of an important change then taking place in the American agricultural sector. The "on-farm" part of America's agricultural economy was shrinking relative to farm input supply industries upstream (seed, farm chemical, and machinery suppliers) and also relative to storage, transport, processing, packaging, marketing, and retail industries downstream. Since farms had become just one part of a lengthening and increasingly industrialized food value chain, it made sense to begin referring to the chain as a single integrated entity: agribusiness.

The new term stuck, a *Journal of Agribusiness* was founded, and soon after, more than 100 institutions of higher education in the United States were offering formal degrees in agribusiness. In 1990, the International Food and Agribusiness Management Association (IAMA) was founded as a worldwide networking organization and bridge among multinational agribusiness companies, researchers, educators, and government officials.

Why is agribusiness controversial?

For those who work inside food and farm industries, the word *agribusiness* is a descriptive term with no bad connotations; in fact, it carries a flattering connotation of modernity. Yet for critics outside the sector, the term carries strongly negative connotations. It is deployed by critics to suggest that traditional and trustworthy family farmers have been replaced by powerful profit-driven corporations not accountable for the damage they do to rural communities, human health, and the environment.

Contemporary critiques of American agribusiness date from 1973, when a Texas populist named Jim Hightower published a book titled *Hard Tomatoes, Hard Times*. The book argued that a consolidation of corporate power over the agricultural sector had subordinated even the U.S. Department of Agriculture and the nation's agricultural universities and was bringing about the demise of small farms, displacing farmworkers, and bringing us unhealthy food. Agribusiness firms were also a target of journalist Eric Schlosser's widely popular 1999 book *Fast Food Nation: The Dark Side of the All-American Meal*. A decade later, in 2009, a popular film titled *Food, Inc.*, asserted that "our nation's food supply is now controlled by a handful of corporations that often put profit ahead of consumer health, the livelihood of the American farmer, the safety of workers and our own environment."

In these popular accounts, specific corporate villains have been identified at every separate link in the value chain. Upstream from farms, chemical companies and multinational seed companies tend to attract the greatest criticism. Here, the St. Louis-based Monsanto Company is often a target because it is both a chemical company (selling herbicides) and a multinational biotechnology company (developing and patenting genetically engineered crop seeds). Immediately downstream from farms, in the handling and shipping of farm commodities, a big private trading company from Minneapolis named Cargill is frequently vilified for its secrecy as well as for its alleged market power. In the meat sector, Tyson Foods, Inc., of Springdale, Arkansas, the world's largest processor and marketer of chicken, beef, and pork, is routinely depicted as an enemy of small family farmers and a threat to the environment. In the packaged food sector, ConAgra Foods, Inc., of Omaha, Nebraska, is said to be damaging consumer health by marketing heavily processed and chemical-laden foods such as frozen dinners, Slim Jims, and Reddi-wip. Finally, at the retail end, the favored targets are fast-food restaurant chains, especially McDonald's and Burger King, accused of addicting our children to obesity-inducing burgers, fries, and sweetened drinks.

Food industries have long been an inviting target for populist attack. In 1906, a muckraking novel by Upton Sinclair, titled *The Jungle*, exposed the disgraceful working conditions in Chicago's meatpacking industry. Like most modern critics of agribusiness, Sinclair was suspicious of corporate motives in general and simply used the emotive and highly personal issue of food to dramatize those larger suspicions. The book caused a sensation, but most readers overlooked the labor rights message and focused instead on a worry that meat products might not be safe to eat. Sinclair's book led directly to passage of the Meat Inspection Act and the Pure Food and Drug Act of 1906 and to the creation of a national Food and Drug Administration (FDA).

Do agribusiness firms control farmers?

Farmers in America have always worried about the market power of nonfarmers. Historically, they worried most about bankers, grain traders, and railroads; today, they worry most about market concentration in the seed industry and the meat-packing industry, where the market power of industry has strengthened considerably.

Concentration in the seed industry has been driven most recently by the patent claims private biotechnology companies are permitted to make in the United States on the seeds they develop using genetic engineering. As of 2008, the Monsanto Company and its subsidiaries owned more than 400 separate plant technology patents. These function as intellectual property claims, enforced in part through contracts farmers sign (stewardship agreements) not to save and replant the seeds after harvest, so they must be bought from the company again the next season. Farmers suspected of violating the terms of this agreement have been sued by the company. The patent claims generally last for 20 years. Watchdog nongovernmental organizations (NGOs) such as the Center for Food Safety point to extreme market concentration in some biotechnology crop sectors. For example, 96 percent of all genetically engineered cotton planted in the United States contains Monsanto's patented traits. Roughly 90 percent of all soybeans planted in the United States are genetically engineered, and 90 percent of the traits belong to Monsanto; 60 percent of corn in the United States is genetically engineered, and more than 90 percent of the traits are Monsanto owned.

Economic studies of the corn and cottonseed industries show, however, that the technology has brought cost-reducing benefits to farmers that outweigh the disadvantage of greater corporate concentration. Farmers buy these seeds voluntarily because the traits can help them cut production costs significantly. Still, Monsanto's temporary commercial monopoly over the patented traits ensures the company will capture a major part of the economic gain. This extreme market concentration grew out of several factors unique to the biotech seed sector. Beyond the opportunity to claim patent rights in some countries (e.g., the United States), the political stigma associated with genetically engineered foods (discussed in chapter 13) has dried up corporate investments in the technology in Europe, leaving Monsanto with few international competitors. Inside the United States, government research money might have been used to develop this technology in the public sector without patent restrictions, but Congress declined, allowing the private sector to take the lead. Monsanto's rivals inside the United States, such as the Iowa-based Pioneer Hi-Bred seed unit of the DuPont Company, press the Department of Justice to initiate antitrust action.

The American meatpacking sector has also become highly concentrated in recent years. As of 2005, four companies controlled the processing of more than 80 percent of the country's beef, and three of those same four companies, along with an additional fourth, processed over 60 percent of the country's pork. Four major companies in broiler chicken processing (including Tyson Foods) now provide more than half of the country's chicken supply. Companies such as Tyson Foods work with thousands of individual "contract chicken growers" who provide their own land and construct the sheds to raise the chickens, while the company owns the chickens and provides all the feed. Both the growers who work for agribusiness firms under this sort of contract and those still struggling to survive as independents have reason to fear that the companies use their market power to gain a disproportionate advantage. In the 1990s, America's hog slaughter industry also moved toward increased vertical integration and concentration, threatening to extend price manipulations even to the market for live hogs still being raised by independent producers. The next worrisome step in vertical integration might take place in cattle markets. A legislative measure to bar meatpackers from owning, feeding, or controlling cattle was inserted into the Senate-passed version of the 2008 farm bill but then dropped in conference before the bill was passed.

In most crop farming outside the biotech seed sector, corporations do not yet have significant market power over farmers. The largest portion of all crop production does come from big farms, yet most of these are still independent family-owned enterprises. Nonfamily corporations account for only 6 percent of all farm sales in the United States. As for control from downstream crop purchasing companies, competitive markets tend to prevail here as well, in part because concentration among the purchasing companies is offset by the countervailing power of farmer marketing cooperatives, which can be formed legally under America's federal marketing order system.

It is a stretch to imagine that international corporations control the lives of poor farmers in the developing world. Most poor farmers in Africa do not make any purchases of seeds at all (they save seeds from the previous season's crop), and they make minimum purchases of fertilizers and pesticides. When they do market a portion of their crop, it is usually to local buyers or to government-regulated marketing boards rather than to vertically integrated agribusiness firms. In Africa, fewer than 2 percent of all investments in agricultural research are made by private firms. The greater danger is not that international agribusiness will control these poor farmers but instead that they will continue to ignore them. Private international companies are not significantly interested in African farmers because they lack the purchasing power to be good customers.

Do food companies and supermarkets control consumers?

Critics suspect that agribusiness firms, including retail super-market chains, exploit their market power to raise the cost of food to consumers. When food prices rose sharply in the United States in the 1970s, Jim Hightower (of *Hard Tomatoes* fame) alleged that without the monopoly power of agri-business, food would have been 25 percent cheaper for the American consumer. Careful studies by economists show that monopoly power in the food manufacturing industry does raise costs to consumers but not by a large percentage. Bruce Gardner, a leading American agricultural economist, calcu-lated that in the 1990s only about 2 percent of the consumer's final marketing bill went to pay for "excess profits" due to imperfect market competition.

With respect to supermarkets, studies show that the industry has become more concentrated and that, in cities with fewer competing stores, consumer food prices are indeed higher. Yet the rate of profit in the retail food industry overall, measured per dollar of sales, has not increased over time thanks to effi-ciencies that accompany larger store size—efficiencies that have largely been passed on to consumers. A study by USDA's Economic Research Service in 1989 found no significant effect on supermarket prices from increasing industry concentration. A review by the Federal Trade Commission in 1990 found the same. Instead of controlling consumers, modern supermar-kets today compete with each other to offer a dizzying range of affordable food purchase options.

Some food companies clearly hold near-monopoly positions for individual food products. For example, General Foods enjoys nearly 90 percent of the market in Jell-O-like products. Yet there is no convincing evidence the company's profits from Jell-O are higher than for products such as peanut butter, where there is much more competition. Whenever profits begin to move up, competitors move in, as in the case of the creatively blended ice cream sold by Ben & Jerry's, which was so successful that it quickly inspired competing alternative brands. The American food industry has roughly 300,000 individual firms overall, more than enough to ensure competition. In the 1970s, the Federal Trade Commission looked at charges that the three largest breakfast cereal companies (Kellogg's, General Foods, and General Mills, which together had 80 percent of the market) were exercising predatory behavior by proliferating their own brands to monopolize store shelf space, but after a 10-year investigation, the case was dropped. In subsequent years, the market share of these top three companies fell, as new private label companies moved into the sector.

Are supermarkets spreading into developing countries?

Supermarkets are pervasive in rich countries, and they are now spreading rapidly into the developing world with uncertain consequences for local food producers.

Supermarkets tend to spread wherever income growth and private automobile ownership are high, wherever women have entered the workforce, and wherever residential patterns have become suburban. North America, Europe, and Japan clearly fit this profile. In France today, just as in the United States, 70–80 percent of national food retail sales are made in supermarkets. More surprising has been the recent and very rapid spread of supermarkets into parts of the developing world where affluence, suburbanization, auto ownership, and female workforce participation are not yet as pervasive. In Latin America, only 10 percent of all food retail sales were made through supermarkets as recently as the 1980s, but by

2000, that figure was up to 50–60 percent. Supermarkets took off 5–7 years later in East and Southeast Asia and then exhibited even faster growth. In Taiwan and South Korea, supermarket sales now have a 63 percent share of all food sales. In China as recently as 1991, there were no supermarkets at all, yet by 2001, the supermarket share in Chinese urban food markets was 48 percent. Supermarkets do not yet serve as many customers in South Asia or in sub-Saharan Africa. For example, retail market shares in India and in Nigeria have recently reached only 5 percent.

One key factor in the spread of supermarkets in poor countries has been electrification and the availability of home refrigerators, which make possible the purchase of fresh foods on a less frequent basis and in larger quantity. Second has been the opening of more national economies in the developing world to foreign direct investment, particularly since the 1990s. This gave established supermarket chains in the United States, Europe, and Japan opportunities to move quickly into the rapidly growing retail food markets of Latin America and Asia. Retail multinationals such as Ahold, Carrefour, Tesco, and Wal-Mart moved quickly once foreign direct investment restrictions were removed. Today in Latin America, the top five international chains have roughly 65 percent of sales in the sector. Three of every ten pesos spent on food in Mexico are now spent at Wal-Mart.

Local food retail stores in developing countries find it hard to maintain their market shares because the multinationals have access to proprietary innovations in logistics and management that allow them to centralize procurement, consolidate distribution, and hence, cut costs. For local consumers, the outcome can be beneficial, as they gain access to a higher volume and variety of food purchase options offered at a generally higher standard for both food safety and cosmetic appearance and at a lower cost thanks to standardization and consolidation. Problems arise, however, for local farmers and also for local food wholesale and retail competitors. Traditional local farmers, small and diversified, cannot provide the steady supply of top quality fresh foods that the multinational supermarkets require.

Traditional growers use inferior harvest techniques and less postharvest product protection, resulting in lower quality produce. As a consequence, they tend to be bypassed by store buyers who contract their procurement instead from modern-style specialty farms that have been created through still more foreign investment. These farms deliver contracted produce either to the supermarket directly or more likely to yet another new commercial institution, a distribution center that will serve as supplier to multiple local supermarkets. Systems of this kind reduce the cost of delivering quality produce to multiple supermarket outlets, but they bypass both traditional local farms and traditional urban wholesale markets, and they are typically foreign owned. The rapid insertion of such exotic systems into traditional food markets in the developing world not only changes the diet of consumers (encouraging the consumption of more packaged foods, processed foods, and internationally branded imported foods), but it also changes the market position of local food producers and wholesalers, keeping their sales away from the most affluent local customer base.

Are fast-food restaurants spreading into poor countries?

Fast-food restaurant chains like McDonald's and Kentucky Fried Chicken are also spreading rapidly into some parts of the developing world, yet the social and dietary impacts are often misunderstood. Fast-food chains went global in the 1980s and 1990s, moving into many of the same countries as supermarkets and at a similarly rapid rate. In 1990, South Korea had 4 McDonald's restaurants; 5 years later, it had 48. In the same short 5-year period, China went from having 1 McDonald's restaurant to 62. Indonesia went from 0 to 38. Brazil went from 63 to 243. During this high-growth period, a new McDonald's restaurant was opening somewhere in the world every 3 hours. Critics of fast food in the United States viewed this as the worst sort of cultural imperialism, going way beyond the pervasiveness of Coca-Cola. The fast-food restaurants were selling entire menus of unhealthy American foods to impressionable young children in poor countries, along with a garish and alien symbolism of smiling clowns and Kentucky colonels.

Anthropologists have now studied the dietary and cultural impact of fast-food restaurants in developing countries, especially in East Asia, and they find the impacts are subtler. In many East Asian settings, fast-food restaurants do not destroy local cuisines because they are usually a place to have a snack between meals or to socialize with friends after school. The food is fast but the eating is not, with many fewer sales made at drive-through pickup windows to on-the-go commuters. Customers in East Asian cities were initially attracted to fast-food restaurants because they had clean restrooms, a feature local restaurants are now under pressure to provide as well.

Asian customers view fast-food chains as distinctly modern, and hence more prestigious, but not always as Western or foreign. In China, McDonald's restaurants are 50 percent Chinese owned, nearly all are managed by Chinese, and 95 percent of the food sold is produced in China. Outside each restaurant, the Chinese flag is hoisted every morning, and surveys even reveal that a majority of the young customers believe Ronald McDonald is Chinese and comes from Beijing. Instead of changing China's family-oriented food culture, McDonald's makes money by catering to it. Entire families are welcomed for celebrations and parties, with paper and pen provided for young children who write and draw. Teahouses and art galleries are common features as well.

McDonald's has also enjoyed rapid growth in India, with 200 restaurants currently in operation and a customer base that increases between 10–15 percent every year. In India, the restaurants also make sales by blending with local food cultures rather than confronting them. In Hindu India, where cows are revered, beef has been taken off the menu and replaced by vegetable patties or by Maharaja Macs made with chicken. In countries such as China and India, growing urban affluence is rapidly changing traditional family life and altering traditional meal patterns. Fast-food chains make money from these changes and speed them along, but the chains did not create the change.

12

ORGANIC AND LOCAL FOOD

What is organic food?

The label *organic* refers to one way food can be produced. Organic foods are produced without any human-made (i.e., synthetic) fertilizers or pesticides. In place of synthetic nitrogen fertilizer to restore soil nutrients, organic farmers use composted animal manure and plant cover crops they can later turn into the soil. In place of synthetic herbicides (weed killers), organic farmers use crop rotations, mechanical cultivation, and mulch. In place of synthetic chemicals to control insects, organic farmers rely on biological controls (birds and beneficial insects that eat bad insects) or on toxins to insects that are naturally occurring, such as *Bt* (from a soil bacterium). Organic farming is not free of toxic chemicals, but the chemicals used must all appear in nature. For example, the insect toxins that can be used include pyrethrins (produced by chrysanthemums) and sabadilla (derived from the ground seeds of lily).

The disciplines for growing food organically are not new, but the widened popularity of organic food among consumers is recent, dating only from the 1990s. Organically grown foods are not to be confused with foods sold as "natural," which earn that name by being minimally processed after growing and free from ingredients such as refined sugar, flour, and food colors or flavorings. It is possible, of course, for foods to be both organic and natural.

What is the history of organic food?

The organic food movement began in Europe early in the 20th century, primarily as a philosophical rejection of synthetic nitrogen fertilizer use. In 1909, two German chemists, Fritz Haber and Carl Bosch, had finally discovered a method to capture atmospheric nitrogen for agricultural use by combining it with hydrogen under high temperature and pressure, resulting in ammonia. Followers of a "vitalist" philosophy, which asserted that living things could only be properly nurtured by the products of other living things (e.g., animal manure), rejected this innovation. The strongest rejection came in Austria, where vitalist mystic Rudolf Steiner (1861–1925) championed what he called *biodynamic* (life force) farming, growing crops with composted animal manure plus other preparations such as chamomile blossom and oak bark. Steiner's approach was later promoted in Germany under the Third Reich by Rudolf Hess and Heinrich Himmler, who had come to doubt the sustainability of using artificial fertilizer and advocated instead "agriculture in accordance with the laws of life."

This early rejection of synthetic nitrogen fertilizers also spread in England, where elements of the aristocracy (including Sir Albert Howard and Lady Eve Balfour) took the lead in arguing against what they considered "artificial manures." To the present day, organic farming has strong support within the English upper class, most notably from

Prince Charles, who in 1986 converted his own Duchy Home Farm to a completely organic system.

The term *organic farming* was only coined later by the American Jerome Irving (J. I.) Rodale (1898–1971), a New York accountant who had taken inspiration from Sir Albert Howard's writings. In 1942, Rodale began a new career publishing a magazine he titled *Organic Gardening and Farming*. Rodale was later also a promoter of alternative healthcare methods and founded *Prevention* magazine in the 1950s.

For several decades, organic farming enjoyed only marginal popularity in the United States, in part because organic products were not available beyond specialty markets or health stores and cost 10 to 40 percent more than conventionally grown products. The organic option gained a new following, however, after Rachel Carson's compelling critique of synthetic pesticide use in her 1962 book, *Silent Spring*. A movement that began as a rejection of synthetic fertilizer was now energized by its parallel rejection of synthetic pesticides. Growing consumer demand plus organic advocacy in the 1980s eventually obliged Congress, in 1990, to mandate the creation of a clear national standard for certifying and labeling organically grown products. It was this credible certification and labeling standard that triggered the recent and rapid expansion of organic product sales.

How is organic food regulated in the United States?

Organic foods are regulated under a National Organic Program (NOP) created in 2002 by the U.S. Department of Agriculture. Under this program, foods can be labeled "organic" only if grown and handled by certified organic producers and processors. The certification is performed not by the USDA directly but by third-party government-accredited certifiers who charge a fee, usually less than $1,000 per farm for initial certification.

Certification is based on a requirement that only "nonsynthetic" substances be used in organic production and handling. Synthetic fertilizers and pesticides are generally prohibited, along with the use of sewage sludge for fertilizer, the use of irradiation to kill food pathogens, and the planting of seeds that have been genetically engineered. The USDA's original proposal would have allowed the use of sewage sludge, irradiation, and genetically engineered seeds, but outraged advocates for organic food sent 275,000 letters of complaint, so the government agreed to exclude all three. Farms must be free of all prohibited substances and practices for at least 3 years to qualify for certification. In animal production, any animals used for meat, milk, or eggs must be fed 100 percent organic food, have access to the outdoors, and may not be given hormones or antibiotics. Certified handlers of food must use only organic ingredients and must prevent organic and nonorganic products from coming into contact with each other. The products marketed by certified growers and handlers are entitled to use a recognized logo, USDA Organic, when labeling their goods.

Once this system began operating in 2002, consumer confidence in the integrity of the organic label increased, and commercial sales of organic products in the United States began increasing rapidly at annual rates of 15–20 percent. Even so, the organic sector remains relatively small in the United States, making up only 2 percent of total food purchases and using only 0.4 percent of U.S. cropland.

Organic purists fear the expansion of organic production has in some ways been too rapid because so much of the expansion came from industrial-scale growers who operate outside the original holistic philosophy of the movement. The purists also mistrust industrial-scale organic growers because they have lobbied to weaken the official organic standard for their own convenience. For example, a 2006 amendment to the organic standard created a list of "synthetic substances allowed for use" in organic crop production over the objections of purists from the Cornucopia Institute and the Organic Consumers Association (OCA). There is nothing in the organic standard to prevent large-scale farms from being certified, so the OCA has to use boycotts in its efforts to discourage consumers from purchasing organic products from what it calls "factory farms."

Is organic food healthier or safer to eat?

Many who buy organic foods believe such foods are healthier than conventional foods because they contain more nutrients. Others believe organic foods are safer to eat because they carry no pesticide residues. Nutritionists and health professionals from outside the organic community tend to question both of these beliefs.

The strongest claim of superior nutrient content has been made by the Organic Center, an institution founded in 2002 to demonstrate the benefits of organic products. In 2008, the Organic Center published a review "confirming" the nutrient superiority of plant-based organic foods, showing they contained more vitamin C and vitamin E and a higher concentration of polyphenols, such as flavonoids. This review was rebutted, however, by conventional nutritionists who showed that the Organic Center had used statistical results that were either not peer reviewed or not significant in terms of human health. Organic milk from cows raised on grass may indeed contain 50 percent more beta-carotene, but there is so little beta-carotene in milk to begin with that the resulting gain is only an extra 112 micrograms of beta-carotene per quart of milk, or less than 1 percent the quantity of beta-carotene found in a single medium-size baked sweet potato.

Most certified health professionals find no evidence that organic foods are healthier to eat. According to the Mayo Clinic, "No conclusive evidence shows that organic food is more nutritious than is conventionally grown food." European experts agree. Claire Williamson from the British Nutrition Foundation says, "From a nutritional perspective, there is currently not enough evidence to recommend organic foods over conventionally produced foods." In 2009, the *American Journal of Clinical Nutrition* published a study, commissioned by the British Food Standards Agency, of 162 scientific papers published in the past 50 years on the health and diet benefits of organically grown foods and found no evidence of benefit. The director of the study concluded, "Our review indicates that there is currently no evidence to support the selection of organically over conventionally-produced on the basis of nutritional superiority." The acidity of organic produce was found to be higher, which enhanced taste and sensory perception, but there was no difference for health.

The claim that organic food is safer due to lower pesticide residues is also suspect in the eyes of most health professionals. The Mayo Clinic says, "Some people buy organic food to limit their exposure to [pesticide] residues. Most experts agree, however, that the amount of pesticides found on fruits and vegetables poses a very small health risk." Residues on food can be a significant problem in many developing countries, where the spraying of pesticides is poorly regulated and where fruits and vegetables are often sold unwashed, straight from the field. Yet in advanced industrial countries such as the United States, this risk is seldom encountered. In 2003, the Food and Drug Administration analyzed several thousand samples of domestic and imported foods in the U.S. marketplace and found that only 0.4 percent of the domestic samples and only 0.5 percent of the imported samples had detectable chemical residues that exceeded regulatory tolerance levels.

What are the tolerance levels? The United Nations, through the Food and Agriculture Organization (FAO) and the World Health Organization (WHO), has established acceptable daily intake (ADI) levels for each separate pesticide. The ADI level is set conservatively at 1/100 of an exposure level that still does not cause toxicity in laboratory animals. Moreover, actual residue levels in the United States on conventional foods are well below the ADI level. For example, when FDA surveyed the highest exposures to 38 chemicals in the diets of various population subgroups, it found that for 4 of these 38 chemicals estimated exposures were less than 5 percent of the ADI level. For the other 34 chemicals, estimated exposures were even lower, at less than 1 percent of the ADI level. Carl K. Winter and Sarah F. Davis, food scientists at the University of California–Davis and the Institute of Food Technologies, conclude from these data, "[T]he marginal benefits of reducing human exposure to pesticides in the diet through increased consumption of organic produce appear to be insignificant."

It is true that conventional foods are sometimes not safe to consume, but organically grown foods can also carry risks. In 2006, bagged fresh spinach from a California farm in its final year of converting to organic certification was the source of *E. coli* infections in the United States that killed at least three and sickened hundreds. In 2009, there were nine documented fatal episodes of salmonella poisoning from peanut butter and ground peanut products traced to peanut plants in Texas and Georgia, both of which had organic certification.

Is organic farming better for the environment?

Organic food is often promoted as "sustainable food" because surface water and groundwater near farms are less likely to be damaged by synthetic pesticide and fertilizer runoff. Against this advantage, however, comes an environmental disadvantage: More land is needed for grazing the animals that will provide the manure for compost, and more land will also be needed to offset the lower yields that are typical for organically grown field crops. In Europe, organically grown cereal crops have yields only 60–70 percent as high as those conventionally grown. In the United Kingdom, organic winter wheat yields are only 4 tons per hectare compared to 8 tons per hectare for conventional farms. If Europe tried to feed itself organically, it would need an additional 28 million hectares of cropland, equal to all the remaining forest cover of France, Germany, Denmark, and Britain combined.

Some environmentally sustainable farming practices cannot be used by farmers who stick to the rigid organic standard. Soil health is often best protected when modest quantities of synthetic chemical fertilizers are used in addition to cover crops, crop rotations, and manure, but the organic standard makes any synthetic nitrogen use impossible. Pest control is best accomplished through integrated pest management (IPM) methods that use chemical insecticides as a judicious last resort in combination with natural biological controls—but once again, the organic standard makes this impossible. The strict prohibition against synthetic herbicide use in organic farming can block the use of modern no-till practices, which are a superior method of avoiding soil erosion and reducing greenhouse gas emissions because they allow more carbon sequestration and less burning of diesel fuel. The organic standard also makes it impossible to plant genetically engineered crops such as *Bt* corn and *Bt* cotton, which have helped conventional farmers reduce insecticide use. These environmental limitations to the organic standard should be unsurprising, since environmental protection was not the original motive for developing organic practices a century ago.

Could the world be fed with organically grown food?

It is no longer possible to feed the world with farming systems that exclude the use of synthetic nitrogen fertilizer. In the past century, the population of Earth has increased from 1.6 billion to more than 6 billion, and these larger numbers have been fed thanks to the higher crop yields made possible by synthetic nitrogen (since the 1930s, wheat yields in conventional farming have doubled). Vaclav Smil, an agronomist from the University of Manitoba, calculates that synthetic fertilizers currently supply about 40 percent of all the nitrogen used by crops around the world. To replace that synthetic nitrogen with organic nitrogen would require the manure production of approximately 7–8 billion additional cattle, roughly a fivefold increase from the current number of 1.3 billion. The United States alone would have to accept nearly 1 billion additional animals and an added 2 billion acres of forage crops to feed those animals, equal to all the land in America except Alaska.

Advocates for organic farming, such as the International Federation of Organic Agricultural Movements (IFOAM), do not address the problem this way. They assert that organic practices can increase yields based on farming projects they have carried out in some of the world's hungriest regions, such as Africa. Organic methods do produce yield gains in Africa if compared to no improved methods at all, but in Africa the most productive methods for restoring soil nutrients usually include a combination of both organic matter and synthetic nitrogen, and the organic standard makes such combinations impossible to use. Organic farming has expanded in Africa recently but mostly to supply export markets (certified organic products destined for supermarkets in Europe) rather than to provide for local food consumption.

Is organic farming a way to save small farms?

Much of the increased appeal of organic farming has come from those who see it as a way to save small farms from a further spread of industrial-scale factory farms. The organic movement in the United States was originally led by a cohort of smaller farmers that grew out of the back-to-the-land movement of the 1960s and 1970s. These organic pioneers usually made their sales directly to consumers either at farm stands and local farmers' markets or through health food stores and subscription services under what came to be known as community supported agriculture (CSA). Yet when the USDA created the national organic standard, farm size and marketing channels were not restricted. Thus, once consumer demand pushed up price premiums for organic products, it was only a matter of time before industrial-scale growers would get in the game, switching to organic methods, becoming certified, and selling through large corporate supermarkets.

Most organic milk, lettuce, and spinach now come from giant corporate operations, and most sales of these products take place in supermarkets. By 2002, only 13 percent of organic vegetable sales in the United States were still being made by small farmers through local farmers' markets. In 2006, Wal-Mart announced it would start offering more organic foods, a move that pulled a number of major commercial food companies—including the manufacturers of Pepsi, Rice Krispies, and Kraft Macaroni and Cheese—into the organic market. These companies source most of their food from large rather than small farms.

What is the local food movement?

The industrial scale of organic farming in the United States has now driven alternative and sustainable food activists to demand something more—*local food*. If food is purchased from local farmers' markets and community gardens, through co-ops, or through CSA subscriptions, it will more likely come from diversified small-scale farms rather than from specialized factory farms. Many of these small local farmers will also be organically certified or at least inclined to rely less on synthetic chemical applications. Survey evidence reveals that the average food buyer is now willing to pay a premium to purchase locally produced foods and twice that premium when buying local food directly from a grower at a farmers' market. The result has been a significant expansion of farmers' markets in the United States—up from 1,755 total in 1994 to 4,385 by 2006. Even so, the vast majority of consumer food purchases continue to be made from nonlocal growers. For every small farmers' market in America, there are still approximately 13 large supermarkets.

Advocates for local food (who call themselves *locavores*) make convincing arguments for the nutritional benefit of buying directly from growers or at farmers' markets. Journalist Michael Pollan, a leading voice for this movement, shows that avoiding supermarkets is one of the best protections against an unhealthy diet of oversalted and oversweetened foods, foods filled with trans fats, elaborately processed and highly preserved foods, and foods designed only for micro-wave ovens. Farmers' markets do not offer these foods, and the produce they do sell is more likely to have been picked recently and picked ripe, ensuring the maximum in both nutri-tional value and taste. Buying food locally also helps preserve open space close to urban centers, and it improves consumer awareness of food production practices.

Supermarkets are now competing for customers by selling foods grown locally, but unlike organic foods there is no single national system for certification, reducing the commercial potential of the market. Labels don't work because the same food product can be local in one market but not local in another. Even agreeing on a single definition of local is difficult. Advo-cates imagine a geography of natural "foodsheds" comparable to watersheds, but the analogy does not go very far because food does not come from the sky and food distribution is not gravity driven. Jessica Prentice, the founder of a community-supported kitchen in Berkeley, California (and the person who coined the term "locavore"), advocates diets consisting of food harvested from within a 100 mile radius—a so-called 100 Mile Diet. This has drawbacks for consumers in climate zones with only a short summer growing season and for consumers in temperate zones who have a taste for tropical products such as bananas or chocolate. "Local when possible" is the sensible rule most advocates settle for in the end.

Locally produced food is unlikely to ever supply more than a small share of the national diet in the United States, given the price-reducing advantages that come from specialization and industrial-scale production in distant locations plus the short growing season in so many regions. The ultimate local food production system, backyard gardening, is culturally popular but also impractical to scale up because of heavy labor requirements, urban residential patterns, and short seasons. In the 20th century, during World War II, the government promoted backyard gardens (victory gardens) to help offset a loss of male farm labor during the war, but even in this extreme instance the backyard gardens were never able to produce more than 40 percent of national vegetable consumption and far smaller shares of other foods. Once the wartime emergency ended, purchases from more distant growers immediately resumed. In 2009, advocates for local food were nonetheless successful in persuading First Lady Michelle Obama to plant a vegetable garden on the White House lawn (something First Lady Eleanor Roosevelt had done in 1943), further popularizing the idea. Backyard gardening was further popularized as a cost-cutting response both to the higher food prices of 2008 and the economic recession of 2009. By one estimate from the National Gardening Association, home food gardening increased 19 percent in 2009 alone.

Does local food help slow climate change?

The claim that locally purchased food contributes less to climate change is not well founded. Reducing "food miles" may be good for freshness, but it will do little to reduce carbon emissions if the local foods are moved about in small quantities rather than in bulk. Bulk shipments of food can be moved over vast distances by rail, barge, or ocean freight with only a small carbon footprint per calorie of food delivered. In contrast, if food is moved about in smaller quantities by pickup truck (or worse, by family automobile), it will have a large carbon foot-print per calorie of food delivered even if it travels fewer miles. If a local farmer drives a small harvest of fresh tomatoes 10 miles round-trip to a farmers' market and if the tomatoes are then purchased a half-dozen at a time and driven an additional 10 miles round-trip by each individual customer, the carbon footprint per local tomato eaten can grow surprisingly large.

Greenhouse emissions from the transport of food off the farm tend to be far less significant than emissions from food production on the farm. Researchers at Carnegie Mellon University have found that of all the greenhouse gases gener-ated by the average U.S. household when it consumes food, the transport of the food accounts for just 11 percent. The best way to reduce the carbon footprint of our diet is not to eat locally but simply to eat less, especially less meat. Eating one less serving of red meat a week achieves the same reduction in emissions as switching to a 100 percent local diet.

Some locally grown foods will also have a much larger carbon footprint on the farm compared to foods transported from a distance. Tomatoes shipped from Mexico in the winter months have a smaller carbon footprint than tomatoes grown locally in a greenhouse. For consumers in the United Kingdom, lamb meat that travels 11,000 miles from New Zealand gener-ates only one-quarter the carbon emissions per ton compared to British lamb because British farmers raise their animals on feed (which must be produced using fossil fuels) rather than on clover pastureland.

What is the difference between local food and slow food?

The *slow-food* movement (logo is a snail) originated in Italy in 1986, initially as a backlash against the introduction of fast foods in Europe. Slow-food advocates seek to preserve local cuisines and gastronomic traditions, including heirloom varieties of local grains and breeds of livestock. They view this as one way to fight back against both the loss of culture and the frenzy brought to us by fast foods, supermarkets, and corporate agribusiness. Slow food is now an important international social movement with roughly 100,000 members organized into more than 1,000 local chapters (called "convivia") worldwide. The United States has far less gastronomic tradition to preserve than Italy, but in 2008, more than 60,000 people attended a slow-food nation gathering in San Francisco, savoring local cuisines at taste pavilions and celebrating the planting of an urban garden in front of city hall.

What explains the loyalty of some groups to organic, local, or slow food?

Societies have always sought solidarity in the foods they eat or foods they agree not to eat. In most religious traditions, patterns of food consumption are carefully regulated. Judaism has strict rules, called *kashrut*, to specify what may and may not be eaten. In Islam, foods are divided into *haram* (forbidden) and *halal* (permitted). Hindus who embrace the concept of *ahimsa* do not eat meat to avoid doing violence to animals. In Roman Catholicism, fasting is required and meat consumption is discouraged at certain times in the religious calendar.

It should not be surprising, in today's more secular age, to find people searching for food rules to follow that express solidarity around secular values. The new rules that emerge (organic, local, or slow) are attractive and practical only for relatively small subcategories of citizens or often for only a small part of the diet of those citizens—but the exclusivity and difficulty of the rule become part of its attraction. The goal is to find and express through the diets we adopt a solidarity with others who share our identity, our values, or our particular life circumstances. The scientific foundation for these modern food rules may be weak, but the social value can nonetheless be strong.

13

FOOD SAFETY
AND GENETICALLY
ENGINEERED FOODS

How safe is America's food supply?

Food in the United States is generally safe and significantly safer than in the past, but the demand for safety has increased as society has become more affluent, creating a parallel demand for improved food safety policy. Food safety lapses are favorite stories in the popular media, and food companies and food retailers can pay a heavy price if the lapse is traced back to them.

More than 200 known diseases can be transmitted through food, caused primarily by viruses, bacteria, parasites, toxins, metals, or prions (as in the case of mad cow disease). The symptoms can range from mild gastroenteritis to life-threatening neurologic, hepatic, and renal syndromes. According to the Centers for Disease Control and Prevention (CDC) in Atlanta, Georgia, food-borne diseases cause approximately 325,000 hospitalizations and 5,000 deaths in the United States each year. Three pathogens, *Salmonella*, *Listeria*, and *Toxoplasma*, are responsible for approximately 30 percent of the deaths. Children under the age of 4 are sickened by food more than any other age group, but adults over the age of 50 suffer more hospitalizations and deaths.

The changing frequency of food-borne illness in any large population is difficult to monitor and measure. Mild cases often go unreported, so official frequency counts are heavily altered by the intensity of surveillance. Nationally since 1996, the CDC has attempted to track food-borne sickness through regular surveys of more than 650 clinical laboratories around the country that serve about 46 million people in 10 different states. At the state level, however, surveillance is less systematic and produces counts that are hard to compare. For example, between 1990 and 2006, the state of Minnesota discovered 548 food-borne illness outbreaks thanks to an aggressive surveillance system, but the state of Kentucky found only 18. Kentucky's food supply was almost certainly not that much safer, if it was safer at all. In some cases, food-borne illness can also be overreported because many pathogens transmitted by food are also spread through water or from person to person without anything being ingested at all. In many cases, the specific pathogens are never identified, creating a further possibility that the illness was unrelated to food.

America's food supply is far safer today than it was in the past, before the era of refrigeration and sanitary packaging. Surveys by the CDC show decades of steadily increasing safety up until 2005, at which point aggregate food safety in the United States reached something of a plateau. One possible explanation for the plateau is that nearly all the easy measures waiting to be taken outside the home had already been taken. The vast majority of all hospitalizations and fatalities today come not from specific outbreaks linked to dangerous batches of contaminated products purchased at supermarkets but instead from a steady background level of illness caused by careless handling and improper preparation inside the home. Unwashed hands, unwashed cutting boards, poorly refrigerated foods, or meats insufficiently cooked can all present serious dangers. Wider illness outbreaks still take place, but the fatalities are usually quite limited. Illness from bagged spinach in 2006 led to a nationwide scare and the virtual suspension of all fresh and bagged spinach sales in America, but there were only three known deaths.

Even if the CDC number of 5,000 annual deaths from food-borne illness is accurate, this is far fewer than from smoking (400,000 Americans a year) or even from obesity (30,000 Americans a year). Note that too much food is now six times deadlier than unsafe food. Yet any illness from foods found already contaminated at purchase will cause public outrage because (in contrast to smoking or overeating) this kind of exposure to risk is involuntary. Also, because purchasing food at supermarkets is a common experience, anxieties can spread quickly to vast numbers of citizens when any danger associated with food purchase is confirmed or even rumored. The unusually wide audience for these fears explains why the popular media give food illness outbreaks from product contamination such sensational coverage. Under the spotlight of this media attention, government officials and politicians find themselves obliged to express intense concern, whatever the actual magnitude of the problem.

How do foods become contaminated?

Food is vulnerable to contamination at nearly every stage in the production and delivery chain, all the way from farm to fork. Microbial contamination of fresh produce is possible at the farm level (a problem with California lettuce and Guatemalan raspberries in the 1990s). In meat slaughter, inadequate knife sterilization and improper evisceration or hide removal can lead to contamination. Pathogens can also be introduced by unsanitary conveyor belts or unclean processing and packaging equipment. Farther down the chain in wholesale and retail outlets, inadequate refrigeration is a problem. In restaurants, cooks who do not wash their hands introduce a risk.

Private industry increasingly seeks to control such contamination through the use of what are called Hazard Analysis and Critical Control Point (HACCP) systems. These systems, first innovated by the Pillsbury Company in the 1960s, identify where hazards might enter into the food production process and specify the stringent actions needed at each separate step to prevent this from occurring. In 1996, the U.S. Department of Agriculture issued a rule for HACCP systems for meat and poultry, requiring systems that are costly for industry, but effective. The USDA estimates that it has cost roughly $310 million since 2000 to reduce *E. coli* 0157:H7 contamination in beef by 50 percent.

Who regulates food contamination in the United States?

At the federal level, food safety responsibility is divided between the Food and Drug Administration (an office of the U.S. Department of Health and Human Services) and the Food Safety and Inspection Service (FSIS), which operates inside the Department of Agriculture. The FSIS is responsible for meat and poultry, and the FDA is responsible for everything else. State public health agencies and city and county health departments also play a continuous monitoring role. Inadequate coordination among these various agencies is a cause for political concern. In 1998, the Clinton administration created a Food Outbreak Response Coordinating Group inside the Department of Health and Human Services, designed to increase communication and coordination. The division of labor between the FSIS and the FDA is particularly problematic. For example, frozen pizzas are inspected by the FDA if they are cheese and by the FSIS if they are pepperoni.

The FDA budget for food inspections is also a partisan issue, with Democrats calling for an increase and Republicans proposing cuts. It is also a problem that the FDA is responsible for both food safety and drug safety, and some have called for a separate agency to oversee food safety exclusively. By 2009, more than a half-dozen food safety policy overhaul bills had been filed in Congress, most designed to give the FDA more financing and greater legal authority to recall unsafe food from the market even without a manufacturer's consent. In 2009, the House of Representatives passed new legislation that contained such a measure and required the FDA to conduct inspections every 6 to 12 months at food processing plants deemed to be high risk. President Barack Obama had described the government's failure to inspect 95 percent of food processing plants as "a hazard to the public health."

Some of this political concern is driven by a dramatic increase in the consumption of imported food. According to the FDA, the volume of FDA-regulated imports doubled between 2003–2008, and 60 percent of these imported shipments were food. Approximately 15 percent of the U.S. food supply is now imported, with the import share for fresh fruits and seafood reaching 50–60 percent of total supply. The FDA can physically inspect less than 1 percent of all food imports because funding levels for this activity were cut by 20 percent between 2002–08. Inspections for high-risk food facilities, including fresh produce firms, declined by a quarter after 2004. The presence of such gaps in government inspection did not prove food had become less safe, but it did fuel intense public suspicion.

Does private industry have sufficient motive and capacity to police itself?

Private industry as a whole has a strong self-interest in food safety. Although the number of Americans likely to be hospitalized with a food-borne illness remains low (roughly 1 in 1,000 every year), costs to private industry can be large following an illness outbreak of any significant size. For example, Hudson Meats was forced out of the industry after being implicated in selling contaminated products, Mexican green-onion exporters suffered a sharp decline in sales after a hepatitis outbreak was traced to their products, and in 2006, American spinach producers experienced a complete loss of sales after the FDA advised consumers to stop eating fresh as well as bagged spinach in the wake of an outbreak of *E. coli* contamination. It was later learned that the contaminated spinach came from just one 50-acre farm and was packaged in one processing plant (and only on one production shift at that plant), yet 3 years later, spinach sales in the United States continued to suffer. Litigation costs are another worry for companies, although many legal cases involving food-borne illness never go forward, and of those that do, only one-third of all plaintiffs receive jury awards. The commercial incentive that industry has to police itself was reflected in the HACCP, which began as a voluntary private initiative. When introducing safety certification plans, private firms often move first, ahead of government regulators.

Incentives for self-policing are weakened, however, by the significant time lag between contaminated product consumption and the onset of illness, which makes it hard to find the specific food source of an illness, and also by the length of the food production, processing, and delivery chain, which makes it hard to trace contamination to a single corporate source.

To strengthen industry's interest in self-policing, larger public investments need to be made in the surveillance and epidemiology of outbreaks and in the traceability of potentially contaminated foods through the production, processing, and delivery chain. As private firms become more certain any serious outbreak will be traced, their voluntary investments in contamination prevention will increase.

Does the industrialization of agriculture make food less safe?

The industrialization of agriculture and the growing scale of most meat and fresh produce processing do not make food more dangerous overall, but they do present new kinds of safety risks. Instead of food contamination outbreaks that are frequent but localized and small scale, the pattern today is outbreaks that are less frequent (per unit of production) yet harder to contain to one local area when they do occur. These nationwide outbreaks quickly attract national media attention, creating an impression that our modern food system has become less safe than the more compartmentalized or localized alternative. The underlying problem with compartmentalized and localized systems is that they tend to be less highly capitalized and thus less able to afford state-of-the-art technical options for food supply protection.

Is irradiated food safe?

One method for reducing or eliminating harmful bacteria, insects, and parasites in food is to irradiate the food with brief exposures to X-rays, gamma rays, or an electron beam. This technology has been known for the better part of a century, yet it remains rarely used in the United States. The Food and Drug Administration approved irradiation as safe and effective for use on poultry in 1992, and on meat in 1997, but the technique is rarely used because it makes the meat more costly and because the industry fears an adverse consumer response to the word *radiation*. In 2001 the CDC estimated that if half the nation's meat and poultry supply were irradiated, the result would be 900,000 fewer cases of food-borne illness and 350 fewer deaths.

Advocates for irradiation observe that the technique has been judged safe by the government and might have killed the salmonella that reached grocery store shelves early in 2009 in peanut butter and peanut paste. Critics say irradiation would only be used by private companies to hide the filthy condition of their plants. These public and political reactions to the irradiation of food tend to mirror, in some ways, public reactions to genetically engineered food.

What is genetically modified food?

Nearly all foods come from plants and animals carrying genes modified over time through human interventions such as seed selection or selective breeding. Yet in current usage, the term *genetically modified* has come to be reserved for plants and animals modified through genetic engineering, also known as transgenic science or recombinant DNA (rDNA) science. Genetic engineering, first developed in 1973, provides a method for modifying plants and animals without sexual reproduction by moving individual genes physically from a source organism directly into the living DNA of a target organism. The power of this technique comes from its precision and from its ability to use a wider pool of genetic resources when pursuing crop or animal modification. For example, genes carrying a trait to resist insect damage can be moved from a soil bacterium named *Bt* into a corn plant or into a cotton plant. The modified versions of these plants are known as *Bt* corn and *Bt* cotton. Alternatively, genes that direct a plant to produce beta-carotene (a precursor of vitamin A, which helps prevent blindness) can be moved from a daffodil plant into a rice plant, resulting in something called "golden rice."

The first engineered crop to be approved for commercial sale was a tomato with extended shelf life (the FlavrSavr tomato), marketed by the Calgene Company in 1994 following regulatory approval by the FDA. Soon after, the Monsanto Company secured approval for the sale in the United States of Roundup Ready soybean plants, which had been engineered to resist the herbicide glyphosate (sold by Monsanto under the trade name Roundup) so as to reduce the cost of weed control. With one application of glyphosate, the weeds would die, but the soybean plants would not. By 1996, Monsanto's varieties of *Bt* corn and *Bt* cotton had also been approved for commercial use in the United States. The European Union then approved a number of genetically engineered crops both for planting and human consumption in 1995–96, including soybean, maize (corn), and canola; Japan approved soybean and tomato; Argentina approved soybean and maize; Australia approved cotton and canola; and in 1995–96, Mexico approved soybean, canola, potato, and tomato.

How are genetically engineered foods regulated?

Each national government has its own system for approving the planting and consumption of genetically engineered crops and foods. The United States, from the start, has regulated genetically engineered crops and foods in much the same manner that it regulates conventional crops and foods, based on a

1987 National Academy of Sciences finding that there was no evidence of "unique hazards" from the modification of plants using rDNA methods versus other methods. All new crops in the United States, including genetically engineered crops, are subject to regulation for biosafety (safety to the biological environment, especially to other agricultural crops and animals) by the Animal and Plant Health Inspection Service (APHIS) of the Department of Agriculture. If a crop has been engineered to produce a pesticide (such as *Bt*), the Environmental Protection Agency (EPA) must give its approval for use. The FDA is the agency that reviews new genetically engineered crops for food safety, and it views genetically engineered varieties of familiar foods as no less safe than conventional varieties of the same foods unless the engineering process has introduced a new or unfamiliar toxicant, nutrient, or allergenic protein into the food. If none of these has been introduced, the technology developers undertake a voluntary consultation with the FDA showing the results of their own safety testing and then put the new product on the market.

Governments in Europe have developed quite a different approach to regulating genetically engineered crops and foods, known there by the label *genetically modified organisms* (GMOs). The European approach is to create separate laws and approval procedures for GMOs and to regulate this technology by a separate and a higher standard. Regulators in Europe are permitted to block the approval of a GMO without any evidence of an actual risk to human health or the environment. Under what is known as the "precautionary principle," a new technology can be blocked simply on a suspicion of new risks or because of a fear that risks not found in the short run could nonetheless develop in the long run.

Despite this more precautionary approach, regulatory authorities in Europe, acting through the European Union, did approve a number of GMO foods and crops along with the United States in 1995–96, as noted earlier. Europe's approach changed after a major health scare emerged in the United Kingdom linked to mad cow disease, which undercut citizen confidence in government food safety regulators. Mad cow disease had nothing to do with GMOs, but European regulators needed to restore their credibility with consumers, so they became more cautious toward all food technologies. In 1998, they imposed an informal moratorium on any new approvals of GMOs, yielding to demands from groups opposed to the technology such as Greenpeace and Friends of the Earth. A number of European governments even began rejecting GMOs completely, including those earlier approved by EU authorities. Finally, in 2004, the European Union introduced a new set of regulations intended to reassure consumers through strict labeling and tracing in the marketplace of any approved GMO foods. Henceforth, all GMO products with as much as 0.9 percent transgenic content would have to carry an identifying label, and operators in the food chain handling approved GMOs would have to maintain an audit trail showing where each GM product came from and to whom it was sold for at least 5 years. These tight regulations were affordable in Europe only because, by then, most GM foods had been removed from the market voluntarily. Supermarket chains, since the late 1990s, had begun competing for customers by promising to be GMO-free.

How widespread are genetically engineered foods?

Since 1995, the global area planted to GMO crops has expanded at double-digit rates every year, reaching 125 million hectares by 2008. Still, the uptake remains geographically limited. As of

2008, only 25 countries around the world contained significant commercial plantings of GMOs, and more than 90 percent of all GMO acreage was confined to five countries: the United States, Argentina, Brazil, India, and Canada. The United States alone makes up half of the total world crop area planted to GMOs. In the United States, at least 70 percent of all foods commercially sold have at least some GMO content. Many consumers are not aware of this, in part because labeling for GMO content is not required in the United States.

Because of consumer anxieties about GMOs, nearly all of the transgenic crops approved so far by regulators have either been industrial crops (e.g., cotton) or crops used primarily for animal feed (e.g., soybeans and yellow corn). As of 2009, the only country to have approved a GM variety of a staple food crop for human use was the Republic of South Africa, which approved the production of a GMO variety of white maize in 2002. Even the United States has so far stopped short of commercializing GMO varieties of staple food crops such as wheat or rice, fearing consumer rejection in foreign markets in Europe and East Asia. Genetically modified potatoes were grown successfully in the United States between 1995 and 1999, but fast-food chains such as McDonald's and Burger King then began to fear activist campaigns against the product, so they asked their suppliers for non-GMO varieties only, and the planting of GMO potatoes in the United States quickly died out.

In Asia as well, GMO varieties of staple food crops have not yet been approved despite the availability of GMO rice plants that have been developed by Chinese and Indian scientists. China and India have been growing GMO cotton commercially since 1997 and 2002, respectively, and the Philippines has approved yellow maize (mostly for animal feed). But as of 2009, not a single Asian country had given approval for the commercial planting of GM rice or wheat.

Reluctance to approve GMOs often grows out of commercial or cultural closeness to Europe. Countries that depend heavily on agricultural exports to Europe or who retain close postcolonial ties to Europe (e.g., countries in Africa) tend to adopt Europe's highly precautionary approach toward the regulation of GMO foods and crops. In Africa as of 2009, the only three countries to have approved the commercial planting of any GMO crops were the Republic of South Africa, Egypt, and Burkina Faso. In the rest of Africa, planting GMO crops is still illegal. Countries in the Western Hemisphere closer to the United States are generally more willing to approve GMOs. As of 2008, seven of the top ten countries with significant plantings of GMOs were Western Hemisphere countries. Geopolitics obviously plays a role. It is not an accident that the only Asian country to have approved GMO maize, the Philippines, was once an American colony.

Are genetically engineered foods safe?

As of 2009, there was not yet any documented evidence of new risks to human health or the environment from any of the GMO foods and crops that regulators had approved for the market. For a new and controversial technology, this stands out as a remarkable safety record. It suggests that the U.S. regulatory system, the one that has been used to approve most of the GMOs currently on the market, has been sufficiently strict—so far, at least—to ensure public safety.

All of the most important scientific academies around the world have concluded that the GMO foods and crops approved by regulators have so far presented no new scientifically documented risks either to human health or to the natural environment. This is now the official position of the Royal Society in London, the British Medical Association, the French Academy of Sciences, the German Academies of Science and Humanities, and the Research Directorate of the European Union. It is also the official position of the International Council for Science (ICSU), the Organization for Economic Co-operation and Development (OECD) in Paris, the World Health Organization (WHO), and the Food and Agriculture Organization (FAO) of the United Nations. It would be possible, of course, to use rDNA to develop an unsafe food (e.g., a soybean with a gene from a Brazil nut that would induce allergic reactions among some unsuspecting consumers), but the scientific consensus says that the regulatory systems currently in place have so far been adequate to screen out such risky technologies.

Skeptics are not convinced by this absence of evidence of new risks. They invoke a precautionary slogan: "Absence of evidence is not the same thing as evidence of absence." Proponents of the technology respond that if you spend a dozen years looking for evidence of a new risk and fail to find any, that may not be proof of absence (because nobody can prove a negative), but it is in fact evidence of absence.

Why is there so much opposition to genetically engineered foods?

Opponents of GMO foods share a range of concerns. Some do not like the technology because it is new and we do not yet know enough about it. Others, especially in Europe, dislike GMOs because most were developed by a U.S. multinational, the Monsanto Company. The fact that the genetic traits in GMOs can be patented in some countries raises a concern about corporate control. For some, the idea of moving genes from one species to another creates ethical discomfort.

Consumer resistance to agricultural GMOs also comes from a deeper source. Consumers find it easy to reject GMO foods and crops because, so far, they have provided almost no direct consumer benefit. Genetically modified soybeans or corn do not taste better, look better, prepare better, or nourish better than conventional soybeans or corn. They are not noticeably cheaper because most of the economic gains from using the technology are captured by the farmer (who saves money by using less insecticide or fewer herbicides) or by the patent-owning biotechnology company. In the absence of any clear new consumer benefit, citizens in rich countries (few of whom are farmers) typically have little to lose when they reject agricultural GMOs.

Where genetic engineering does deliver a clear benefit, citizens tend not to reject this new science. For example, there is virtually no social resistance either in Europe or in the United States to recombinant medical drugs made from genetically engineered bacteria or from the genetically engineered ovary cells of Chinese hamsters (despite the fact that these drugs are also patented and also sold by profit-making American multinationals). Several important differences explain this more welcoming social response. Most important is the fact that GMO drugs can deliver clear benefits to most citizens in rich countries, but the first generation of GMO agricultural crops provided benefits only to farmers, seed companies, and patent holders. Also, medical GMOs are physically contained within laboratories, so they arouse no environmental anxieties, whereas agricultural GMOs are released as living things into the natural environment. Finally, recombinant drugs are always labeled and prescribed by a physician with the patient's knowledge, but agricultural GMOs were first introduced into the food supply without mandatory labels, making consumers uncomfortable about involuntary exposure.

Another reason for social opposition to agricultural GMOs has been a widespread disinformation campaign waged against the technology by opposition groups. Critics of GMOs have asserted, without evidence, that the new crops cause more spraying of herbicides rather than less, and are more likely than conventional crops to result in pesticide-resistant insects or invasive superweeds. Scientific authorities such as the International Council for Science have discredited these charges, yet they continue to be made. Another charge is that pollen from GMO corn kills monarch butterfly larvae, but studies conducted by the EPA revealed that under field conditions the risk is "negligible" because the exposure of monarch caterpillars to *Bt* corn pollen is almost always below a level that could cause any harm. Yet the assertion continues to be made.

Another bogus yet widely circulated assertion is that GMO crops contain *terminator genes*, which render the seeds sterile. A patented technology does exist that could produce sterile seeds, but this technology has never been used in any of the GMO crops now on the market, so the seeds have been just as easy for farmers to replicate as the seeds of conventional crops. In fact, the technology has often spread into new countries, such as Brazil and India, by farmers who freely replicated and replanted them. It is true that GMO seeds can be patented in some countries, including the United States and Canada, and farmers in these countries must sign a pledge not to replicate the seeds and to instead buy new seeds every year. Yet this kind of patent protection does not exist in any of the countries of Asia or Africa, so small farmers there would never face such restrictions.

It has also been asserted that GMO crops are so prone to failure that the purchase of GM seeds has driven cotton farmers in India deep into debt, leading to an upsurge in farmer suicides. An independent investigation of this charge revealed that farmer suicides had not increased in India since the introduction of *Bt* cotton and that the technology was in fact highly popular overall and was spreading rapidly because it performed extremely well.

Food safety risks have also been asserted against GMOs. In Britain in 1998, the media gave loud play to the results of a laboratory experiment in which GMO potatoes were fed to rats, supposedly with damaging health effects, but the Royal Society later issued a statement saying it was wrong to conclude anything from the experiment due to flaws in its design. The results have never been replicated by scientists using a proper study design, yet the media attention given to this case played an important early role in driving up consumer anxieties. Critics later warned that eating GMO foods would result in a transfer of antibiotic resistance genes into the human body but again without any sound experimental verification. In 2002, one UK organization named Farming and Livestock Concern went so far as to warn officials from the government of Zambia that it would be unwise to accept GMO maize from the United States as food aid because inside the human body it could form a retrovirus similar to HIV. The Zambians were concerned and decided to refuse the food aid. A more recent charge emerged from a study done in Austria in 2008 that purported to find lower reproduction rates among mice that had been fed with GMO corn. When the Scientific Panel on Genetically Modified Organisms of the European Union reviewed the study, it found calculation errors, inconsistencies in treating the data, and an error in the method of calculating numbers of young mice (per pair rather than per delivering pair), which it said nullified any conclusions that might be drawn from the study. Yet critics of GMOs continue to cite this study in the popular media.

Can genetically engineered foods help solve global hunger?

The first generation of GMO crops that came onto the market was designed primarily to make weed and insect control less expensive for temperate zone commercial farmers growing soybeans, corn, and cotton. The fit of these crops to the needs of poor smallholder farmers in tropical countries was not particularly close. Small cotton farmers in both China and India have been able to benefit from planting *Bt* varieties of cotton, but in tropical Africa, the crops small farmers tend to grow—such as sorghum, millet, banana, cassava, and yams—are not currently available to them in a genetically engineered form. Private biotechnology companies have little commercial incentive to invest in the engineering of improved varieties of these crops because farmers in Africa are too poor to become good seed-buying customers. One solution to this problem would be to rely less on private companies and return instead to public sector agricultural research, carried out through the Consultative Group on International Agricultural Research (CGIAR; a network of publicly funded international agricultural research centers) or within national agricultural research systems (NARS) in individual countries in Africa. However, the international controversies surrounding GMO foods and crops have discouraged the use of public money for this purpose. As of 2007, only 3 percent of the CGIAR budget went toward any research on GMOs.

Some second generation applications of genetic engineering to agricultural crops could be a much better fit to poor country needs, such as rice plants engineered to be higher in beta-carotene (golden rice) to help address vitamin A deficiencies in poor countries or corn plants engineered to do a better job of surviving under drought conditions. Yet private biotechnology companies like Monsanto have little incentive to invest in these technologies for the poor, and public funding to develop these technologies has been hard to find due to political controversy. Research funded by the Rockefeller Foundation led to the creation of golden rice in 2000, a dramatic scientific breakthrough that made the cover of *Time* magazine, but GMO critics attacked the project, and due to political resistance, another 8 years passed before the first field trials in a developing country, the Philippines, could be conducted. It is not yet legal in any developing country for farmers to plant golden rice. Research on drought-tolerant GMO varieties of tropical white maize, intended to help poor farmers in Africa, gained funding by the Bill and Melinda Gates Foundation in 2008 after the project had been turned down by public sector funders. Yet due to the uncertainties of getting government permission to conduct any GMO field trials in most of Africa, the benefits of this project will probably not be available to a significant number of farmers in tropical Africa until well past the year 2015. Planting GMO crops is still illegal in nearly all of Africa. Farmers in the United States are expected to be planting GMO drought-tolerant corn by 2012, but farmers in Africa, who have a much greater need for this technology, will not get it until much later, if at all.

14

WHO GOVERNS THE WORLD FOOD SYSTEM?

Why aren't there stronger authorities to govern food and farming around the world?

International governance in the area of food and farming remains weak because the power of separate national governments remains strong. In many other sectors, due to increased cross-border flows of people, goods, services, and money, the power of national authorities is under challenge, and this has led to the emergence of more powerful transnational and intergovernmental institutions above the nation-state. Meanwhile, in sectors such as information technology and communications, the power of the nation-state is being challenged from below, as individuals within society find themselves more empowered to resist state authority. Yet in the food and farming sectors, national governmental institutions continue to play a dominating role in both rich and poor countries.

Food and farming systems have distinct traits that give national governments a political advantage over other institutions. First, most food and farming systems remain significantly local or, at most, national in terms of geography. Most of the world's food continues to be grown, harvested, processed, retailed, and consumed entirely within national borders.

This is particularly true for large states. China imports only 0.5 percent of its total wheat and coarse grain consumption. In all of South Asia, only 1 percent of total rice consumption is imported. Some countries do import a significant share of their bulk commodity consumption; for example, the countries of the Middle East import more than 33 percent of their cereal consumption (an increase from just 15 percent in the 1970s), but processed food markets in particular are still largely national. The U.S. Department of Agriculture estimated in 2005 that only 10 percent of global processed food sales ever entered international trade.

Food and farming systems also tend to remain under the power of separate nations because they are built so heavily around immobile assets, such as agricultural land and irrigation water. For such assets, claims of territorial sovereignty can be used to prevent global governance institutions or transnational corporations from taking control. Food and farming systems also tend to remain nonglobalized because of differing agroclimatic conditions across world regions, which lead to diverse cuisines and highly distinctive systems of farming and eating country by country.

The instruments used by national governments to exercise control over food and farming systems differ between rich and poor countries. In rich postagricultural (increasingly, postindustrial) societies, farming tends to be heavily shaped by income subsidies to producers, import restrictions at the border, tax credits to farmers, and public investments in research and water system infrastructure. It is not unusual to find a significant share of the total farm income dependent on public policy (30 percent in the European Union, on average, and 52 percent in Japan). Off the farm, food systems in rich countries are heavily shaped by national industrial competition policies (e.g., antitrust) and by a wide range of regulatory systems (e.g., for food safety or for environmental protection).

In poor countries, state intervention in the agricultural production and marketing sector tends to be more pronounced, and less often pro-farmer. In much of Asia, the management of spatially extensive irrigation systems has long been an excuse for heavy state intervention in farming. National programs governing the ownership and distribution of agricultural land (including periodic efforts at redistribution under the slogan of "land reform") are also a government prerogative. State subsidies for everything from fertilizers and pesticides to electricity for irrigation pumps continue to play a large role. State-run marketing systems that make commodities available to the poor through fair price shops are not uncommon. In a few developing countries, such as North Korea, everything remains in the public sector.

In much of Africa, elements of the national commodity production and marketing systems first created under colonial rule still survive, operated today through state-owned enterprises or "parastatal" institutions that have been granted monopoly rights by the government. Agricultural sectors in these developing countries are more open to import competition and to foreign direct investment than they were in the past, but globalization has lagged in the farm sector due to weak rural infrastructure—bad roads and little electrical power.

Which international organizations do play a governance role?

Some international organizations do exercise influence over food and farming sectors. One example is the World Trade Organization (WTO), originally created as the General

Agreement on Tariffs and Trade (GATT) at an international conference in Bretton Woods, New Hampshire, in 1944. The WTO is headquartered in Geneva, where it provides a setting in which national governments can negotiate agreements on trade policy, including agricultural trade policy and the domestic farm policies that distort international trade. The WTO has a Dispute Settlement Body (DSB) that adjudicates claims from member governments regarding the noncompliance of states with these international agreements, and agricultural policies (e.g., cotton policy in the United States or sugar policy and GMO regulations in the European Union) have often been the triggers for such claims. Deliberations within the DSB draw on the findings of one other international institution, the Codex Alimentarius ("food code") Commission in Rome, a body created by the United Nations in 1963 to develop common global standards for safe food products and fair food trade practices. Because Codex traditionally operates by consensus, common global standards in controversial areas such as GMOs have not been achieved.

The International Monetary Fund (IMF) and the World Bank (IBRD) are two other international institutions created at Bretton Woods in 1944. They are largely funded by wealthy country governments and empowered to make sizable loans to governments in developing countries, particularly those facing financial crises or struggling to create a policy environment for sustained economic growth. The lending conditions typically imposed by the IMF include market deregulation and an end to inflationary fiscal and monetary policies. The World Bank in the 1960s and 1970s became a significant source of lending for investments in agricultural development, but over the following three decades, it cut its lending to agriculture and moved on to other concerns. Following the high world food prices of 2008, World Bank president Robert Zoellick vowed to revive lending for agriculture. The IMF and the World Bank are both headquartered in Washington, D.C., and have traditionally embraced a so-called Washington consensus that emphasizes the role of free markets and private investments as opposed to state planning, market controls, and government subsidies.

In addition to Codex Alimentarius, three other significant international food and agricultural organizations can be found in Rome, all part of the UN system. The youngest of these, the International Fund for Agricultural Development (IFAD), was established in 1977 to finance development projects that focus specifically on food production and rural poverty alleviation. The IFAD is less constrained by the Washington consensus than either the IMF or the World Bank. The second Rome organization, the UN World Food Programme (WFP), was established in 1961 to manage the delivery of humanitarian food assistance to poor countries and to refugee populations. Individual donor governments are still the source of nearly all international food aid, but more than half of that aid is now channeled to its destination by the WFP. The oldest and most prominent Rome-based UN institution is the Food and Agriculture Organization (FAO). Founded in 1945, the FAO devotes most of its energy today to gathering and distributing information about food and farming around the world. It also provides a forum for nations to meet to set goals, share expertise, and negotiate agreements on agricultural policy. The FAO has been host to several prominent world food conferences in recent decades—in 1974, during the first world food crisis; then again, in 1996; and once again in 2008 and 2009, responding to the most recent food price crisis. At FAO, the agricultural ministries of member governments are typically in the lead, so the organization often places greater emphasis on agricultural producers than on food consumers.

In the area of agricultural technology development and research, the most important international institution is the Consultative Group on International Agricultural Research (CGIAR), a network of research centers created in 1971 and chaired by the World Bank. The CGIAR eventually expanded into a network of 15 separate international agricultural centers, mostly located in the developing world and funded by government donors and private foundations, plus the World Bank. These centers attempt to carry and extend the legacy of the original green revolution of the 1960s and 1970s, using science to develop improved seeds and more productive farming methods to help farmers still struggling with low productivity.

How powerful are these international organizations?

The political influence of these international food and agricultural institutions remains quite limited. Negotiations in the WTO, for example, have so far had only a small impact on the farm subsidy policies that distort trade. The obligations that emerged from the most recently completed round of WTO negotiations (the Uruguay Round in 1986–93) were so weak that they forced neither the United States nor the European Union to undertake any subsidy reductions beyond those being imposed anyway for other reasons, such as domestic budget constraints. This 1993 Agreement on Agriculture did require industrial countries to convert nontariff agricultural border protections to tariffs, but the new tariffs were set so high that in some cases they implied an increase, not a reduction, in permitted border protections, a practice that came to be called "dirty tariffication." The agreement imposed no restriction at all on most of the cash payments to farmers that both the United States and the European Union used as their key subsidy instrument. The agreement also did nothing about restrictions on food exports, such as those that worsened the sudden international food price increases of 2008. The continuing failure of the more recent Doha Round of negotiations (launched in 2001) to go beyond this weak Uruguay Round outcome is further evidence of the WTO's political limitations.

Even when governments agree to some policy restrictions under the WTO, they do not always comply. For example, in 2005, the United States was told by the Dispute Settlement Body that elements of its cotton subsidy program were illegal under the terms of the 1993 Agreement on Agriculture, but the United States refused either to change its policies adequately or pay compensation. Then in 2008, the U.S. Congress passed a new farm bill that explicitly retained some of the offending cotton policies.

The IMF and the World Bank have also had limited influence. These lending agencies attempted in the 1980s to employ "structural adjustment" programs to pressure developing country governments into reducing their policy interventions in the food and farm sectors, but the results were not always significant or long-lasting. In 1994, the World Bank completed a study of 29 governments in sub-Saharan Africa that had undergone structural adjustment and found that 17 of those 29 had reduced the overall tax burden they placed on farming, but some, because of persistently overvalued exchange rates, had actually increased that burden. Only 4 of the 29 had eliminated parastatal marketing boards for major export crops, and

none of the 29 had in place both agricultural and macroeconomic policies that measured up to World Bank standards.
Later, the International Food Policy Research Institute (IFPRI)
found in a study that many of the reforms undertaken in
response to World Bank pressures were reversed following
external shocks or when economic conditions changed.

The World Bank diminished its own influence over agriculture when it cut the total value of its lending in that sector
beginning in the 1980s. Between 1978 and 1988, the share of
lending from the World Bank that went to agricultural development fell from 30 percent to 16 percent, and by 2006, the
lending share was down to only 8 percent. In 2005, World Bank
president Paul Wolfowitz admitted in an offhand comment,
"My institution's largely gotten out of the business of agriculture." To explain this withdrawal of lending for agriculture,
officials at the World Bank claimed that borrowing country
governments had changed their priorities, yet priorities at the
bank had changed as well. Structural adjustment lending for
policy change had crowded out lending for actual investments
in development.

Of the Rome-based UN food organizations, the WFP and
IFAD are frequently praised for their work, and the FAO
is frequently criticized. The WFP has a proven record of
preventing famine, as in the case of the 1991–92 drought in
southern Africa when 17–20 million people were at risk.
Thanks in part to the WFP's timely solicitation of food aid
donations and its effective channeling of aid deliveries, no
famine deaths were recorded except in Mozambique, where
the aid could not be delivered because a civil war was under
way. Drought returned to southern Africa in 2001–02, this time
putting 15 million people at risk, and once again, the WFP was
able to solicit and deliver enough aid to prevent famine.

The WFP nonetheless depends entirely on national govern-ments for access to those in need and for the aid it delivers. Donor governments are sometimes slow with their pledges, and recipients sometimes refuse to grant access. The WFP has yet to convince the biggest donor, the United States, to adopt the best practice of making contributions in the form of cash rather than commodities, and it has been blocked from doing its job at various times by rogue regimes, such as those in Myanmar and North Korea.

The FAO has a much weaker reputation for effectiveness. In fact, it was frustration with FAO during the world food crisis of the 1970s that led to the creation of the IFAD in 1977. The data collection activities of FAO are highly regarded, and in some niche areas (e.g., the integrated management of crop pests, or IPM), its technical advice has been world class, but its operations often are too heavily dominated by an oversized headquarters bureaucracy under the lethargic direction of unresponsive leaders who hold their positions more because of their political allies than their professional competence. This pattern is found in many UN special agen-cies, but at FAO, the problem is particularly severe. Too many FAO resources never leave the city of Rome. A recent internal review timidly recommended that FAO set as a goal to locate at least 40 percent of its staff and spend at least half of its budget outside Rome.

The research centers of the CGIAR have had a four-decade history of success in developing useful new farm technolo-gies for the developing world. The improved rice varieties originally developed by the International Rice Research Insti-tute (IRRI) have now been released in more than 77 countries, allowing the world to more than double total rice production since 1965. Two-thirds of the developing world's total area planted to wheat is now planted to varieties that contain improvements developed by the CGIAR's International Maize and Wheat Improvement Center (CIMMYT). Nevertheless, the CGIAR has struggled for the past two decades to hold onto adequate donor funding, due partly to complacency among those who thought the world's food production problems were already solved plus hostility from others who rejected the green revolution approach. The CGIAR's methods have not always been ideal; too much crop science at the centers is conducted under artificial conditions rather than in farmers' fields, and too often the new technologies developed never reach the intended beneficiaries. Extending new production technologies to poor farmers is a task that almost always requires strong institutions at the national level.

How much power do international NGOs have?

International nongovernmental organizations (NGOs) are increasingly influential players on the world stage, and they exert a notable influence both in the food and the farming sectors. Some NGOs work almost exclusively through projects on the ground. For example, Heifer International operates nearly 900 projects in 53 different countries to promote food self-reliance through gifts of livestock and training. Other NGOs work almost exclusively through advocacy. Greenpeace, an environmental advocacy organization based in Amsterdam, maintains chapters in 68 countries with approximately 1,200 full-time staff. Consumers International, a global federation of more than 230 advocacy organizations in 113 different countries, promotes consumer food safety. Some NGOs work almost exclusively as subcontractors for national development ministries, so they are nongovernmental in name only. In Norway, for example, 22 of 70 international NGOs engaged in development work obtain more than 80 percent of their budget from the national government. National budgets are the source of 85 percent of international NGO funding in Sweden, 80 percent in Belgium, and 66 percent even in the United States.

In the area of food safety and farm technology, advocacy NGOs are often successful in exposing and even blocking behaviors they do not like. In the 1970s, a network of NGOs accused the Nestlé company of promoting infant formula products through unethical methods, such as giving away free samples in maternity wards. An NGO-led boycott of Nestlé products, driven by the charge "Nestlé Kills Babies," led eventually to a new International Code of Marketing of Breast-milk Substitutes that Nestlé pledged to follow in 1984. Also in the 1980s, an international NGO advocacy campaign led by the Pesticides Action Network (PAN) produced an International Code of Conduct on the Distribution and Use of Pesticide and later a binding international agreement, the Rotterdam Convention. In the 1990s, two European-based international NGOs, Greenpeace and Friends of the Earth, successfully promoted an agreement (the Cartagena Protocol) under the Convention on Biological Diversity that now restricts international trade in living agricultural GMOs, known as LMOs (an LMO is nothing more than the living seed or the viable plant material of a genetically engineered plant).

Not all NGOs engage in oppositional advocacy. Some food security NGOs, like Bread for the World, use information as well as advocacy campaigns to promote food aid and agricultural development. Others, like Oxfam, mix information and advocacy with projects on the ground. Still others, like Mercy Corps, work almost exclusively delivering humanitarian relief. In the area of agricultural development, however, there are clear limits to what NGOs from the outside can accomplish on their own. They can deliver excellent training services in medicine, education, and technology adoption, but they are less able to provide investments that might be badly needed in road construction, electricity, irrigation, and agricultural research. National government must take that lead.

One limitation of international NGOs is their tendency to export the concerns of rich countries to developing countries. In areas such as health and human rights, this can be entirely appropriate, but with agricultural technology, the concerns of the rich are not always well matched to the needs of the poor. Agricultural chemical use is clearly excessive in Europe and North America, but many NGOs carry their campaigns against chemical use into Africa, where too little fertilizer is used rather than too much. At a 1996 FAO World Food Summit in Rome, international NGOs agreed to promote traditional technologies and organic farming in the developing world. In fact, most smallholder farmers in Africa are currently using traditional techniques, and many are de facto organic because they purchase almost no chemicals, yet they are hardly productive or prosperous. Five years later at a follow-up UN food conference, the international NGOs reconvened and asserted that the green revolution was responsible for a rise in world hunger, an implausible conclusion because the only part of the world experiencing increased hunger was sub-Saharan Africa, the region least touched by green revolution seeds and practices.

What is the role of private foundations?

Independently endowed philanthropic foundations such as the Rockefeller and Ford Foundations played an essential role in launching Asia's original green revolution in the 1960s and 1970s. The single most important foundation engaged in food security around the world today is the Bill and Melinda Gates Foundation.

The Ford Foundation, with roughly $10 billion in assets, is an important New York–based institution that provided early support to the green revolution in Asia but has more recently moved away from promoting science-based approaches to farming. The Rockefeller Foundation has an endowment only one-third as large as Ford, but it remained an important source of support for agricultural science in developing countries long after Ford abandoned the cause. Then in 2006, the much larger Bill and Melinda Gates Foundation began supporting work in agricultural development, originally through a $150 million joint venture with Rockefeller called the Alliance for a Green Revolution in Africa (AGRA), chaired by former UN Secretary General Kofi Annan. The main thrust of this initiative was an across-the-board effort to improve the varieties of seed available to small farmers for staple food crops in Africa.

By invoking the phrase "green revolution," the Gates foundation knew it would be inviting criticism from those in the NGO community who mistrusted high-yield, science-based farming, and soon after the foundation announced its new effort, an NGO based in the United States named Food First warned that Bill and Melinda Gates were "naïve about the causes of hunger" and that their efforts would only provide "higher profits for the seed and fertilizer industries, negligible impacts on total food production and worsening exclusion and marginalization in the countryside." Wishing to avoid such hostile criticism from NGOs, many in the philanthropic community shy away from doing traditional agricultural development work.

Is development assistance from rich countries an answer to hunger in Africa?

Hunger afflicts roughly one-third of all people in sub-Saharan Africa. It is particularly acute in rural areas, where 60 percent of all Africans struggle to feed their families while working as farmers, growing crops and herding animals. Because these people—women, mostly—tend to be lacking in nearly everything they would need to be more productive (most have no improved seeds, no irrigation, no fertilizers, no machinery, no electrical power, no veterinary medicine, and no vehicles or paved roads for transport), their crop yields are only about one-tenth to one-fifth as high as in rich countries, and they earn only about $1 a day. It is the low productivity of their land and labor as farmers that keeps them poor and leaves them vulnerable to hunger.

The solution to this problem must include larger public investments in rural development by governments in Africa. Investments are needed in rural roads and transport infrastructure, rural power, rural water projects, agricultural research, and the extension of productive new technologies to farmers. Unfortunately, because of the urban bias that affects regimes in Africa, too little of this public investment has been made, so the productivity of farming continues to lag even as population continues to increase. In per capita terms, sub-Saharan Africa is producing 14 percent less maize today than it did in 1980. The total number of undernourished people in Africa has roughly doubled since 1980, and under a business-as-usual scenario, this number will increase by another 30 percent by 2020.

This growing problem of hunger, linked in Africa to low farming productivity, has until recently brought forth surprisingly little in the way of development assistance from the outside world. Donor governments have responded to Africa with more food aid rather than more aid to farmers. The United States allowed its official development assistance to agriculture in Africa to fall from more than $400 million annually in the 1980s to only $60 million by 2006, a decline of approximately 85 percent. During that same time, America's food aid budget for Africa more than doubled in real terms, up to $1.2 billion. In other words, the United States was spending roughly 20 times as much giving away food in Africa as it was spending to help Africans do a better job of producing their own food.

At least three political factors had combined to push the United States away from providing adequate assistance for agricultural development. First, the enormous success of the original green revolution on the irrigated lands of Asia in the 1960s and 1970s left a false impression that all of the world's food production problems had been solved. In fact, on the nonirrigated farmlands of Africa, these problems were just beginning to intensify. Second, the Washington consensus doctrine developed inside the International Monetary Fund and the World Bank in the 1980s had also influenced Congress and the U.S. Agency for International Development. Under this doctrine, the job of the state was mostly to stabilize the macroeconomy and then get out of the way, hoping private investors and private markets would then create more wealth. This approach failed in rural Africa because the basic public goods needed to attract private investors and help markets function—roads, power, and an educated workforce—had not yet been provided.

Finally, a new fashion also arose beginning in the 1980s among advocates for social justice and environmental protection. These groups began to argue that agricultural modernization could be dangerous: Only large farmers would profit, and increased chemical use would harm the environment. Once again, this perspective did not fit Africa, where fertilizer use was too low rather than too high and where nearly all farmers were smallholders with adequate access to land. Yet under the influence of such views, U.S. assistance to agriculture in poor countries—including those in Africa—declined. Other donor governments then pulled back as well, and the aggregate value of all bilateral agricultural development assistance from all rich countries to all poor countries fell by 64 percent between 1980 and 2003.

The shock of temporarily high world food prices in 2008, followed by the inauguration of Barack Obama as president in 2009, led to a revival of donor support for agricultural development, or at least promised support. Several months after taking office, President Obama pledged to double U.S. agricultural development assistance up to more than $1 billion by 2010, and at a summit meeting of the G8 countries in Italy in July 2009, Obama convinced the world's wealthy nations to make a collective pledge of $20 billion over 3 years to promote food security and agricultural development in poor countries. Skeptics noted that not all of the money pledged was new money, and they remembered earlier G8 assistance pledges that had not been fulfilled, but the protracted period of diminished external assistance to agriculture appeared at last to be ending.

It is hard to say what role this long interlude of diminished assistance has played in Africa's worsening food crisis. Africa's own governments must accept primary responsibility due to their own underinvestments in the productivity of small farmers, but the multidecade withdrawal of support by donors made the problems worse. Either way, it was national governments that had been responsible, and it was national governments that had failed to deliver.

GLOSSARY

agribusiness: The large private companies that now provide inputs to farmers (seed, chemicals, machinery) and that handle farm products on their way to the final consumer (transport, processing, packaging, wholesale, and food retail companies).

Agricultural Adjustment Act (AAA): The 1933 act of Congress that first created commodity-by-commodity income support programs (subsidies) for American farmers under President Franklin D. Roosevelt at the depths of the Great Depression.

agroecological approaches: Farming methods promoted as an alternative to standardized high-yield farming, based instead on the knowledge of local communities and working with nature rather than through the domination of nature, claimed by advocates to be better for social justice and environmental sustainability.

American Farm Bureau Federation: Known as the Farm Bureau, a national organization that lobbies in Congress for the interests of large commercial farmers (most of them Republicans).

biodynamic farming: A precursor to modern organic farming developed by an Austrian philosopher and mystic named Rudolf Steiner (1861–1925), using "life force" methods rather than synthetic chemicals such as nitrogen fertilizers.

biofuels: Transportation fuels made from plants, such as ethanol made from sugar or corn, diesel fuels made from vegetable oil, or cellulosic ethanol made from nonedible plant parts.

body mass index (BMI): A measure of the roundness of the human body, based on body weight in kilograms divided by the square of height in meters. People with a BMI above 25 are considered overweight, and those with a BMI above 30 are considered obese.

calorie deficit: Eating and drinking less caloric energy than the body burns off through basic metabolism and muscular exertion, resulting in weight loss.

cash crop: Crops grown to be sold by the farmer rather than grown to be consumed on the farm.

chronic undernutrition: A sustained calorie intake deficit or a sustained intake deficit of micronutrients such as iron, zinc, iodine, or vitamin A, resulting in wasting, stunting, lethargy, reduced cognitive function, and vulnerability to illness.

Codex Alimentarius: A "food code" commission in Rome, created by the United Nations in 1963 to develop common global standards for safe food products and fair food trade practices, based on consensus (a procedure that often results in an absence of agreed standards due to political controversy).

command economy: A political system that uses central planning and governmental authority to guide production and consumption rather than price signals set through market competition.

Conservation Reserve Program (CRP): A voluntary feature of American agricultural policy that uses federal money from the Commodity Credit Corporation (CCC) to pay eligible farmers yearly "rental fees" to take a portion of their land out of production for 10 to 15 years.

Consultative Group on International Agricultural Research (CGIAR): A network of 15 international research centers, most located in the developing world, chaired by the World Bank, and funded by government donors and private foundations, working to develop improved seeds and more productive farming methods in the tradition of the original green revolution of the 1960s and 1970s.

desertification: The degradation of land in dry regions, principally caused when a combination of wind and drought plus excessive animal grazing kills or removes the plants that hold the soil.

ethanol: Identical to the pure alcohol found in alcoholic beverages, a fluid derived from sugar or maize (corn) for use as a biofuel, burnable by conventional automobile engines when blended with ordinary gasoline.

eutrophication: A degraded condition in water systems caused by too many plant nutrients (e.g., from nitrogen fertilizer runoff) leading to plant and algae growth and then, in the end, to a lack of oxygen for fish and other aquatic species once the plant life dies and decomposes (a process that uses up oxygen).

exchange entitlement: In the usage of economist Amartya Sen, a way of getting food by exchanging something for it (either goods, labor, or the wages earned from labor) rather than hunting or growing the food without any exchange (described by Sen as a direct entitlement to food).

fallow time: The length of time a piece of farmland is allowed to remain idle without a planted crop; a means to help restore soil nutrients in a traditional farming system of shifting cultivation.

famine: A severe food emergency that is specific in both place and time (e.g., the Bengal famine of 1943), in which significant numbers of people die either from starvation or because severe calorie intake deficits have left them weakened and vulnerable to disease.

farm bill: The legislative measure passed by Congress every 5 years or so that renews income subsidies for American farmers plus food assistance programs for poor consumers.

farm lobby: A loose collection of private organizations representing multiple groups of farmers (large farmers, small farmers, dairy farmers, wheat growers, sugar producers, corn growers, etc.) that lobbies members of Congress to enact a new farm bill every 5 years or so, delivering subsidies and other legislated benefits to the American farm sector.

farm subsidies: Government subsidies intended to boost the income of farmers that take the form of direct cash payments, trade protection from foreign competitors, market interventions to raise farm commodity prices, or exemptions from some kinds of taxation.

food aid: The international shipment of food not through commercial channels but through "concessional" channels, as a gift from a donor government to a recipient government, from a donor to a nongovernmental organization, or to a multilateral organization such as the World Food Programme (WFP) of the United Nations.

Food for Peace Program: The oldest United States food aid program, established in 1954 under Public Law 480, which began as a means to dispose of surplus government-owned stocks of wheat.

food miles: The distance an item of food travels between where it is produced and where it is finally consumed, with each added mile decreasing the freshness of the food and, in some cases, increasing its carbon footprint.

food power: An exercise of coercive power based on a manipulation of international food trade, usually a threat by the government of an exporting country to reduce or terminate either commercial exports or food aid to an importing country government.

foodshed: A term, borrowed imprecisely from the concept of a watershed, used by advocates of more localized food systems to describe the "flow" of food from where it is grown to where it is consumed.

genetically modified food: Food that contains ingredients from crop plants developed using the modern science of genetic engineering, also known as transgenic or GMO crop plants, including most of the soybean and corn plants currently grown in the United States.

Global Hunger Index: A composite measure of chronic undernutrition constructed by the International Food Policy Research Institute (IFPRI), combining country-by-country measures of the prevalence of caloric intake deficits, the prevalence of wasting or stunting among children under age 5, and rates of child mortality.

global reserve stocks: A tally of the total tonnage of food commodities (especially wheat, rice, and maize) still in storage (public or private) at the end of each year, just before the new harvest begins.

GMO: A label favored in Europe for genetically modified organisms, or agricultural crop plants developed using genetic engineering (a somewhat arbitrary label because conventional plant breeding also modifies crop genes).

green revolution: The introduction of new high-yield varieties of wheat and rice into developing countries in Asia and Latin America in the 1960s and 1970s, leading to a dramatic increase in staple food production.

Grocery Manufacturers Association: An association of American companies that manufacture food and beverage products, dedicated to promoting the interests of those companies through public relations and government lobbying at both the federal and state levels.

hidden hunger: Damaging (but hard to notice) undernutrition caused not by calorie intake deficits but instead by too little intake of micronutrients such as vitamins and minerals.

intercropping: A practice of planting more than one kind of crop in a field at the same time during the same growing season—for example, planting a row of beans between rows of maize.

International Assessment of Agricultural Knowledge, Science and Technology for Development (IAASTD): This 2008 assessment emerged from an ambitious multiyear, multistakeholder process under the auspices of the United Nations, intending to map both the past and future impacts of agricultural technology on hunger, poverty, nutrition, human health, the environment, and society.

International Food Policy Research Institute (IFPRI): An international research center (part of the CGIAR system) located in Washington, D.C., that engages in independent analysis of the consequences (primarily, the economic consequences) of different government policies in the food and agricultural sectors, primarily in developing countries.

LMO: A living GMO—for example, the viable seed of a GMO agricultural plant (rather than a seed that has been milled or cooked for food).

local food: Food that is grown or raised relatively close to the final consumer—for example, within 100 miles.

locavore: A person who believes in the importance of eating local food.

micronutrient deficit: An inadequate intake of vitamins and minerals, such as a niacin deficiency (causing pellagra), a vitamin D deficiency (causing rickets), or an iron deficiency (causing anemia).

monetization: A controversial practice of selling food aid commodities into local food markets in poor countries to raise revenues for local development projects.

National Farmers Union: Known as the Farmers Union, a national organization that lobbies in Congress to promote the interests of smaller farmers (most of them Democrats).

national food balance approach: A crude means to estimate food availability nationwide, based on a calculation of annual production plus imports plus stocks minus consumption and exports.

National Organic Program (NOP): A program created in 2002 by the U.S. Department of Agriculture to certify producers and processors of foods that are organically grown.

no-till: A method of planting and protecting crops from weeds without disturbing (plowing or tilling) the soil.

obesity: A condition of being seriously overweight, calculated as a body mass index (BMI) higher than 30.

organic food: Basically, food that has been grown, raised, and processed free from any contact with human-made substances, such as synthetic nitrogen fertilizers or synthetic pesticides.

precision farming: Farming that guides machinery and applies inputs such as chemicals and water with greater precision through the use of advanced technologies such as a Global Positioning Systems (GPS), lasers, or computer-controlled drip irrigation.

slow food: A social movement that began in Italy in the 1980s in reaction to the introduction of fast-food restaurants into Europe, advocating the preservation and enjoyment of traditional local cuisines based on heirloom varieties of crops and animals.

subsistence economy: An economy in which most families provide for their own food, clothing, and shelter in contrast to a cash or credit economy more heavily dependent on buying and selling in a commercial marketplace.

sustainable agriculture: Methods of agricultural production that do not ignore looming problems on the farm (e.g., soil nutrient depletion, falling levels of groundwater for irrigation, or a growing resistance to chemicals in the pest population) and that do not shift environmental burdens onto others in society—for example, by releasing polluting chemicals into the air and water.

sustainable food: A term sometimes used by advocates of local and organic food to make the claim that these forms of agriculture are more sustainable (environmentally and in other ways) than conventional farming.

terminator genes: A term used by critics of genetically engineered crops to assert the claim, which is erroneous, that the seeds of such crops have been engineered with special genes that make them sterile.

UN Food and Agricultural Organization (FAO): A specialized UN organization located in Rome that gathers and shares information on food and farming around the world and provides national governments (especially national ministries of agriculture) with a venue to meet to discuss food and farm issues.

UN World Food Programme (WFP): A specialized UN organization located in Rome that channels humanitarian international food aid from donor governments to recipients in the developing world facing emergencies such as drought or civil conflict.

U.S. Agency for International Development (AID or USAID): The agency of the U.S. government that is most directly responsible for managing development assistance and other programs of foreign aid in the developing world.

victory garden: Originally, the home gardens for vegetables widely planted by ordinary citizens in the United States during World War II to make up for farm labor diversions during wartime. Backyard gardens are now promoted by the local food movement.

LIST OF ACRONYMS

(AAA)	Agricultural Adjustment Act of 1933
(ACRE)	Average Crop Revenue Election Program
(ADI)	Acceptable daily intake
(AFBF)	American Farm Bureau Federation
(AGRA)	Alliance for a Green Revolution in Africa
(AOA)	American Obesity Association
(APHIS)	Animal and Plant Health Inspection Service
(BMI)	Body mass index
(CAFO)	Concentrated animal feeding operation
(CAP)	Common Agricultural Policy
(CDC)	Centers for Disease Control and Prevention
(CGIAR)	Consultative Group on International Agricultural Research
(CIMMYT)	International Maize and Wheat Improvement Center
(CPR)	Common property resource
(CRP)	Conservation Reserve Program
(CSA)	Community supported agriculture
(DSB)	Dispute Settlement Body
(EPA)	Environmental Protection Agency
(FAO)	UN Food and Agriculture Organization
(FDA)	U.S. Food and Drug Administration

(FEWS)	Famine early warning system
(FSIS)	Food Safety and Inspection Service
(GATT)	General Agreement on Tariffs and Trade
(GDP)	Gross domestic product
(GHI)	Global Hunger Index
(GIS)	Geographical Information System
(GMA)	Grocery Manufacturers Association
(GMO)	Genetically modified organism
(GPS)	Global Positioning System
(HACCP)	Hazard Analysis and Critical Control Point
(HFCS)	High-fructose corn syrup
(IAASTD)	International Assessment of Agricultural Knowledge, Science and Technology for Development
(IAMA)	International Food and Agribusiness Management Association
(IATP)	Institute for Agriculture and Trade Policy
(IBRD)	International Bank for Reconstruction and Development, known as the World Bank
(ICSU)	International Council for Science
(IFAD)	International Fund for Agricultural Development
(IFOAM)	International Federation of Organic Agricultural Movements
(IFPRI)	International Food Policy Research Institute
(IMF)	International Monetary Fund
(IPM)	Integrated pest management
(IRRI)	International Rice Research Institute
(ISAA)	International Size Acceptance Association
(LISA)	Low-input sustainable agriculture
(LMO)	Living modified organism
(NAAFA)	National Association to Advance Fat Acceptance
(NAFTA)	North American Free Trade Agreement
(NARS)	National agricultural research systems

(NFU)	National Farmers Union
(NGO)	Nongovernmental organization
(NOP)	National Organic Program
(NRA)	National Restaurant Association
(OCA)	Organic Consumers Association
(OECD)	Organization for Economic Co-operation and Development
(PAN)	Pesticides Action Network
(PETA)	People for the Ethical Treatment of Animals
(rDNA)	Recombinant DNA
(SNAP)	Supplemental Nutrition Assistance Program
(USAID)	U.S. Agency for International Development
(USDA)	U.S. Department of Agriculture
(WFP)	UN World Food Programme
(WHO)	World Health Organization
(WIC)	Special Supplemental Nutrition Program for Women, Infants, and Children
(WTO)	World Trade Organization

SUGGESTIONS FOR FURTHER READING

Food Production and Population Growth

Diamond, Jared. *Collapse: How Societies Choose to Fail or Succeed*. New York: Penguin, 2005.

Falcon, Walter P., and Rosamond L. Naylor. "Rethinking Food Security for the 21st Century." *American Journal of Agricultural Economics* 87, no. 5 (2005): 1113–27.

Lappe, Frances Moore, and Joseph Collins. *Diet for a Small Planet*. New York: Ballantine Books, 1971.

Malthus, Thomas Robert. *An Essay on the Principle of Population*. Cambridge: Cambridge University Press, 1992.

Paddock, William, and Paul Paddock. *Famine, 1975! America's Decision: Who Will Survive*? Boston: Little, Brown, 1967.

United Nations. *World Population Prospects 2002: Analytical Report*. New York: United Nations, 2004.

World Bank. *World Development Report 2008: Agriculture for Development*. Washington, D.C.: World Bank, 2007.

The Politics of High Food Prices

Food and Agriculture Organization of the United Nations. *The State of Food Insecurity in the World: High Prices and Food Security—Threats and Opportunities*. Rome: Food and Agriculture Organization of the United Nations, 2008.

Mitchell, Donald O., Merlinda D. Ingco, and Ronald C. Duncan. *World Food Outlook*. New York: Cambridge University Press, 2008.

Pardey, P. G., J. M. Alston, and R. R. Piggott (eds.). *Agricultural R&D in the Developing World: Too Little, Too Late*? Washington, D.C.: International Food Policy Research Institute, 2006.

United States Department of Agriculture, Economic Research Service. *Food Security Assessment, 2007*. Outlook Report No. GFA-19, Agriculture and Trade Reports. Washington, D.C.: United States Department of Agriculture, 2008.

Von Braun, Joachim. *Responding to the World Food Crisis: Getting on the Right Track*. Washington, D.C.: International Food Policy Research Institute, 2008.

The Politics of Chronic Hunger

Akhter U. Ahmed, Ruth Vargas Hill, Lisa C. Smith, Doris M. Wiesmann, and Tim Frankenberger. *The World's Most Deprived: Characteristics and Causes of Extreme Poverty and Hunger*. 2020 Discussion Paper 43. Washington, D.C.: International Food Policy Research Institute, 2007.

Kotz, Nick. *Hunger in America: The Federal Response*. New York: Field Foundation, 1979.

Lipton, Michael. *Why Poor People Stay Poor: Urban Bias in World Development*. Cambridge, Mass.: Harvard University Press, 1977.

Oxfam International. *Causing Hunger: An Overview of the Food Crisis in Africa*. Briefing Paper 91. Oxford, UK: Oxfam, 2006.

Sachs, Jeffrey D., John McArthur, Guido Schmidt-Traub, Margaret Kruk, Chandrika Bahadur, Michael Faye, and Gordon McCord. "Ending Africa's Poverty Trap." *Brookings Papers on Economic Activity* 1 (2004): 117–240.

Smith, Lisa C., and Lawrence Haddad. *Overcoming Child Malnutrition in Developing Countries*, Discussion Paper 30 (February). Washington, D.C.: International Food Policy Research Institute, 2000.

United States Department of Agriculture. "How Many U.S. Households Face Hunger...and How Often?" *Amber Waves*, Economic Research Service/USDA, 2, no. 1 (February 2004): 7.

The Politics of Famine

Becker, Jasper. *Hungry Ghosts: Mao's Secret Famine*. New York: Holt, 1998.

Conquest, Robert. *Harvest of Sorrow: Soviet Collectivization and the Terror Famine*. New York: Oxford University Press, 1987.

Grada, Cormac O. *Famine: A Short History*. Princeton, N.J.: Princeton University Press, 2009.

Haggard, Stephan, and Marcus Noland. *Famine in North Korea: Markets, Aid, and Reform*. New York: Columbia University Press, 2009.

Natsios, Andrew. *The Great North Korean Famine*. Washington, D.C.: United States Institute of Peace Press, 2002.

Sen, Amartya. *Poverty and Famines: An Essay on Entitlement and Deprivation*. New York: Oxford University Press, 1983.

The Green Revolution Controversy

Altieri, Miguel. *Agroecology: The Science of Sustainable Agriculture*. 2nd ed. Boulder, Colo.: Westview Press, 1995.

Evenson, R. E., and D. Gollin. "Assessing the Impact of the Green Revolution, 1960 to 2000." *Science* 300 (May 2003): 758–62.

Hayami, Yujiro, and Vernon W. Ruttan. *Agricultural Development: An International Perspective*. Baltimore, Md.: Johns Hopkins University Press, 1985.

Hazell, Peter, and Lawrence Haddad. *Agricultural Research and Poverty Reduction*. Food, Agriculture, and Environment Discussion Paper 34. Washington, D.C.: International Food Policy Research Institute, 2001.

Hazell, Peter, C. Ramasamy, and P. K. Aiyasamy. *The Green Revolution Reconsidered*. Baltimore, Md.: Johns Hopkins University Press, 1991.

International Assessment of Agricultural Science, Technology, and Development. *Executive Summary of Synthesis Report*, 2008. http://www.agassessment.org/docs/IAASTD_exec_summary_JAN_2008.pdf.

Ruttan, Vernon W. "Controversy about Agricultural Technology: Lessons from the Green Revolution." *International Journal of Biotechnology* 6, no. 1 (2004): 43–54.

Williams, Robert G. *Export Agriculture and the Crisis in Central America*. Chapel Hill: University of North Carolina Press, 1986.

Food Aid and Food Power

Barrett, Christopher B., and Daniel G. Maxwell. *Food Aid after Fifty Years: Recasting Its Role*. New York: Routledge, 2005.

Hanrahan, Charles E. *International Food Aid Provisions of the 2008 Farm Bill*. Congressional Research Service Report for Congress, July 10, 2008.

Paarlberg, Robert. *Food Trade and Foreign Policy: India, the Soviet Union, and the United States*. Ithaca, N.Y.: Cornell University Press, 1985.

The Politics of Obesity

Kessler, David A. *The End of Overeating*. Emmaus, Pa.: Rodale Press, 2009.

Ludwig, David S. "Childhood Obesity—The Shape of Things to Come." *New England Journal of Medicine* 357, no. 23 (2007): 2325–27.

Popkin, Barry. *The World Is Fat*. New York: Penguin, 2008.

The Politics of Farm Subsidies and Trade

Anderson, Kym. "Reducing Distortions to Agricultural Incentives: Progress, Pitfalls, Prospects." *American Journal of Agricultural Economics* 88, no. 5 (2006): 1135–46.

Deere, Carolyn, and Daniel Esty (eds.). *Greening the Americas*. Cambridge, Mass.: MIT Press, 2002.

Food First. *Food Sovereignty: A Right for All—Political Statement of the NGO/CSO Forum for Food Sovereignty*. Oakland, Cal.: Food First, June 14, 2002.

Gardner, Bruce L. *American Agriculture in the Twentieth Century: How It Flourished and What It Cost*. Cambridge, Mass.: Harvard University Press, 2002.

Honma, Masayoshi, and Yujiro Hayami. "The Determinants of Agricultural Protection Level: An Econometric Analysis." In *The Political Economy of Agricultural Protection*, edited by Kym Anderson and Yujiro Hayami. Sydney: Allen and Unwin, 1986.

Orden, David, Robert Paarlberg, and Terry Roe. *Policy Reform in American Agriculture: Analysis and Prognosis*. Chicago: University of Chicago Press, 1999.

Paarlberg, Robert. *Fixing Farm Trade: Policy Options for the United States*. New York: HarperCollins, 1987.

Tracy, Michael. *Government and Agriculture in Western Europe 1880–1988*. 3rd ed. New York: New York University Press, 1989.

Agriculture, the Environment, and Farm Animals

Carson, Rachel. *Silent Spring*. Boston: Houghton Mifflin, 1962.

Cline, William. *Global Warming and Agriculture: Impact Estimates by Country*. Washington, D.C.: Peterson Institute, 2007.

Masson, Jeffrey. *The Face on Your Plate: The Truth about Food*. New York: W. W. Norton, 2009.

Organization for Economic Cooperation and Development. *Environmental Performance of Agriculture in OECD Countries since 1990*. Paris: 2008. www.oecd.org/tad/env/indicators.

Paarlberg, Robert. *Countrysides at Risk: The Political Geography of Sustainable Agriculture*. Baltimore, Md.: Johns Hopkins University Press, 1996.

Smaling, Eric, Moctar Toure, Nico de Ridder, Nteranya Sanginga, and Henk Breman. *Fertilizer Use and the Environment in Africa: Friends or Foes?* Background paper, African Fertilizer Summit. Abjua, Nigeria: June 9–13, 2006.

Steinfield, Henning, Pierre Gerber, Tom Wassenaar, Vincent Castel, and Mauricio Rosales. *Livestock's Long Shadow: Environmental Issues and Options*. Rome: Food and Agriculture Organization of the United Nations, 2006.

Agribusiness, Supermarkets, and Fast Food

Belasco, Warren. *Appetite for Change: How the Counterculture Took on the Food Industry, 1966–1988*. New York: Pantheon, 1989.

Grey, Mark A. "The Industrial Food Stream and Its Alternatives in the United States: An Introduction," *Human Organization* 59, no. 2 (Summer 2000): 143–50.

Reardon, Thomas, C. Peter Timmer, and Julio Berdegue. "The Rapid Rise of Supermarkets in Developing Countries." *Journal of Agricultural and Development Economics* 1, no. 2 (2004): 168–83.

Watson, James. *Golden Arches East: McDonald's in East Asia*. 2nd ed. Stanford, Cal.: Stanford University Press, 2006.

Organic and Local Food

Counihan, Carole. *Food Culture: A Reader*. 2nd ed. Routledge, 2007.

Fromartz, Samuel. *Organic, Inc*. New York: Harcourt, 2006.

McWilliams, James E. *Just Food*. Boston: Little, Brown, 2009.

Pollan, Michael. *The Omnivore's Dilemma: A Natural History of Four Meals*. New York: Penguin, 2006.

Ronald, Pamela C., and Raoul W. Adamchak, *Tomorrow's Table: Organic Farming, Genetics, and the Future of Food*. New York: Oxford University Press, 2008.

Smil, Vaclav. "Global Population and the Nitrogen Cycle" *Scientific American* (July 1997): 76–81.

Smil, Vaclav. *Enriching the Earth, Fritz Haber, Carl Bosch, and the Transformation of World Food Production*. Cambridge, Mass.: MIT Press, 2001.

UNEP-UNCTAD. *Organic Agriculture and Food Security in Africa*. Capacity-Building Task Force on Trade, Environment and Development. New York and Geneva: United Nations, 2008.

Vogt, G. "The Origins of Organic Farming." In *Organic Farming: An International History*, edited by W. Lockeretz, 9–29. CABI, 2008.

Williamson, Claire. "Is Organic Food Better for Our Health?" *Nutrition Bulletin* 32, no. 2 (2007): 104–8.

Winter, Carl K., and Sarah F. Davis. "Organic Foods." *Journal of Food Science* 7, no. 9 (2006): 117–24.

Food Safety and Genetically Engineered Food

Brookes, Graham, and Peter Barfoot. *GM Crops: The Global Socioeconomic and Environmental Impact—the First Nine Years 1996–2004*. Dorchester, UK: PG Economics, October 2005.

Huang, J., R. Hu, C. Fan, C. E. Pray, and S. Rozelle. "*Bt* Cotton Benefits, Costs, and Impacts in China," *AgBioForum* 5 no. 4 (2002): 153–66. http://www.agbioforum.org.

James, Clive. *Global Status of Commercialized Biotech/GM Crops*. ISAAA Brief 39. Ithaca, N.Y.: International Service for the Acquisition of Agri-biotech Applications, 2008.

Jasanoff, Sheila. *Designs on Nature: Science and Democracy in Europe and the United States*. Princeton, N.J.: Princeton University Press, 2005.

Mead, Paul S., Laurence Slutsker, Vance Dietz, Linda F. McCaig, Joseph S. Bresee, Craig Shapiro, Patricia M. Griffin, and Robert V. Tauxe. *Food-Related Illness and Death in the United States*. Atlanta, Ga.: Centers for Disease Control and Prevention, 2000. www.cdc.gov/ncidod/eid/vo15no5/mead.htm.

Paarlberg, Robert. *The Politics of Precaution: Genetically Modified Crops in Developing Countries*. Washington, D.C.: International Food Policy Research Institute, 2001.

Paarlberg, Robert. *Starved for Science: How Biotechnology Is Being Kept Out of Africa*. Cambridge, Mass.: Harvard University Press, 2008.

Who Governs the World Food System?

Chicago Council on Global Affairs. *Renewing American Leadership in the Fight against Global Hunger and Poverty*. Chicago: Chicago Council on Global Affairs, 2009.

Easterly, William. *The White Man's Burden: Why the West's Efforts to Aid the Rest Have Done So Much Ill and So Little Good*. New York: Penguin, 2007.

Keck, Margaret E., and Kathryn Sikkink. *Activists beyond Borders: Advocacy Networks in International Politics*. Ithaca, N.Y.: Cornell University Press, 1998.

Paarlberg, Robert. *Governance and Food Security in an Age of Globalization*. Food, Agriculture, and the Environment Discussion Paper 36. Washington, D.C.: International Food Policy Research Institute, 2002.

INDEX